THE
SECOND
SPRING
PART I

THE SECOND SPRING

PART I

by

C.O. Abear, AB.
E.M. Abear, M.D.

LEGAIA
BOOKS

Legaia Books™
555 Fayetteville Street
Suite 201 Raleigh, NC 27601
www.legaiabooks.com
info@legaiabooks.com
Phone: (704) 216-4194

The Second Spring: Part 1
C.O. Abear, A.B. & E. M. Abear, B.S. M. D.

Published by Legaia Books & C.O. Abear, A.B. & E. M. Abear, B.S. M. D. 8/31/2017

ISBN: 978-1-946946-72-0 (sc)

Any people depicted in stock imagery provided by Thinkstock are models, and such images are being used for illustrative purposes only.
Certain stock imagery © Thinkstock.

This book is printed on acid-free paper.

DEDICATION

This book is lovingly dedicated to Engr. Rolando Bachiller and Arhlene Bachiller who built the St. Michael's Monastery to house the Sisters of the Society of the Angels of Peace.

Engr. Bachiller translated my life long earned pension to a beautiful monastery, where the sisters pray for peace in the world.

And my appreciation to Arhlene Abear Bachiller for being by the side of her husband, Rolly throughout the construction of the monastery in Argao Cebu, Philippines.

FOREWORD

The purpose of this book is to raise money to donate to Mother Angelica of the EWTN in Irondale, AL, Sister Mary Siena Bracero, S.A.P. of the St. Michael's Monastery in Argao, Cebu, Philippines and to Sister Leonie A. Minoza of the Medical Mission, Manila, Philippines.

THANK YOU.

By: C.O. Abear, A.B. & E. M. Abear, B.S. M. D.

PREFACE

This book is a compilation of extraordinary experiences of the authors and contributors that depict God's unfailing love.

The articles, letters, and various testimonies written here are based on true stories, which could be viewed as defining moments and turning points of one's faith.

Nowadays, with the adversities and unfathomable events taking place, faith in God could be shaken, leading us all to question God's role in our lives. Even in our mundane lives, we tend to undermine God's hand working for our good, for the greater good.

It is the purpose of this book to remind us of God's magnificence and loving kindness. As we look forward to our second spring of life, may we thread this journey with trust and confidence, that the Almighty God has our fate in his hands.

Wherever we are in our lives right now, if we only believe in God, even in the simplest of things, we can find His miracles taking place. May this book increase your faith and rekindle the seeds of hope in your heart.

- Mary Grace Antonette Abear, B.A., B.S.c.,M.S.,
Marriage and Family Therapist Intern, and
Professional Clinical Counselor Intern.

Table of Contents

THE SECOND SPRING

The second spring is my second birth after I lost my first spring, a life everlasting in the garden of Paradise, a priceless legacy squandered by our first parents, Adam and Eve (*Genesis 1-3, 15 foll*). This story seems to echo from long ago, so distant now that even though the event is part of the Word of God, it has become to some of us, a fairy tale.

Lest you misunderstand, this is not about the *natural evolution of my second childhood*. But, it is about how I have been undergoing my *second spring*. I might be at the doorstep since I am 79 years old. But by God's grace, my life is on hold by His divine providence. Alleluia!

Let me remind you that the **second childhood** is the age we all understand. It is similar to but not the same as the gift of Down Syndrome. It is the age of innocent wonderment in a "**new**" world of its own, no longer fully aware of the "**old**" world we once enjoyed when our youth was in full flower.

This is the natural result when man's brain shrinks in old age. To some, it gives way to second childhood. You asked: *"What is your name?"* You got the answer: *"I live in the Philippines."*

This is about **my second spring** (our second spring) which through the grace of God, complete with long memory and "variable" short memories of the present have come, through spiritual transformation, by <u>knowing God and the lives of Saints</u>, showing me the beauty and grandeur of the epiphany of my second birth. Let me spell this out more clearly before semantic confusion sets in:

COMMERCIAL: It took me ten (10) volumes to write about THE SECOND SPRING. My attempt in this brief article is only a snap shot, a bird's eye view of what to expect from the age of reason till the age of faith at 79 years old. It is the story of how I managed to keep my journey on this narrow road less taken by some.

To start, just as the first childbirth is the birth into earthly life, the anticipation of which is a celebration of great joy. Death too is literally the 2nd childbirth into a heavenly life the happiness of which God said, *"No ears have heard nor eyes have seen… the Mansion that I have prepared for you." (John 3: 1-2)*

If it were not so, our earthly life would have *no purpose and meaning*. In that context, one would understand why some people might think their famous motto is *"Drink and be merry for tomorrow you die."* Dr. Charles Norwood, once said to me, "10:1" is the ratio of rich people who would commit suicide, as compared to "1:10" for the poor.

In other words, these are wealthy people who have enjoyed their earthly life to the full so much so that upon seeing no purpose in life, they kill themselves – sadly that's the "**successful**" achievement of *The Prince of* *darkness*. In contrast, the poor appear to kill themselves mostly due to **economic hardship**. *They forget the life of St. Joseph, the foster father of Jesus.*

Therefore, let us not waste our time over this dismal outlook of life for common sense as G. K. Chesterton said, "*is uncommon*" among this type of people. Let us recall what Rick Warren wrote, man's intense desire is to seek the only *TRUTH who is Christ.* For Christ is the Truth, the Way, and the Life.

Do you remember what Christ said, "*Unless you are born again as one of these little children you cannot enter the gate of Heaven?" (John 3:1-2)*. Hence, if we must have our "**2ⁿᵈ childbirth**" into eternal life, we should be like children to God.

When we are truly sorry for our sins when we are at the brink of death (barring presumptive motive) Christ said, "*Your soul though as scarlet in sin, it shall be made white as snow." (Isaiah 1:18)*. I am aware that you might have a different interpretation. But simply put, let me just share with you that before God we are only his little children to whom we say: "Our Father."

Yes, *our Father who art in Heaven (Matthew 6:9-13)*. Though His kingdom is in Heaven, we can still find Heaven on earth as St. Therese, *the little Flower*, found Heaven on earth by doing ordinary things with extraordinary perfection. She died a Saint at age 24 and as a Doctor of the Church: I am ashamed to think of that, never mind my age.

The bottom line is: *Heaven is the other people.* That is, the *kingdom of God shall come* down on earth when we can bring our Heaven to other people by loving them the way our Father in Heaven loves us. Yet, we too can bring our Hell to other people when our heart is full of anger and pride.

Remember, a person can only give what grace he has, if God dwells in him.

Our life therefore is a **second spring** if by the grace of God, we are constantly shedding our sinfulness by humble confession to the priest who acts in loco Christi. So, that one day when we die, we are ready to regain what our first parents, Adam and Eve lost, our life eternal in paradise, our **first spring**.

Let me share with you how I have been shedding my own sinfulness. To start, I once hated people. Hate made them live in my mind and heart. Worse than you could imagine: I murdered and raped people in my mind. But Christ told me like a little child, *"Love your neighbor as you love yourself." (John 13:34)*

Yet, no matter how I had tried to be good in this life, it was not surprising that there were people who hated my guts and wanted me to slip on a banana peel. As Jesus showed his ultimate goodness by dying on the Cross, we should not wish anyone to slip on a banana peel.

Anyway, at age 79 I desire to die soon. Who should not wish so, when out of 14 brothers I am left alone, which would be - not to mention - a relief to some, but a grief to a few who loved me. If I therefore say that I want "**to die soon**," one factor that must have convinced me is that having work so hard for many years until age 79, I could say at age 79: *My Lord, I am finished; I am done.*

And if life has no purpose and meaning, I could understand why some rich people would jump into the Niagara Fools. I mean, Niagara Falls. Why? There is no place for God in the heart of self-serving people. To them God would say, *"What does it profit a man if he gains the whole world and at the end suffer the loss of his own soul." (Matthew 16:26)*

When St. Francis Xavier, a famous good-looking young philosophy teacher at the University of France, heard that statement from St. Ignatius Loyola, he gave up his worldly life and obeyed what he said, *"Go and set the world on fire (for Christ's sake)."*

And he did. He arrived in Lanao, Mindanao. **Tradition** says that since St. Francis could not convert the Muslims, he threw his boot in desperation into Lanao lake before going to Japan - and a horse island emerged. See it for yourself.

This happened in spite of the "fact" that the Datu, of the Muslims, after he hid his 2 lovely daughters, challenged St. Francis that if he could tell what was in his basement, he would be converted. Without hesitation St. Francis said, "You got nothing but 2 pigs." Hence, from that day on, the Datu passed a law prohibiting good Muslims not to eat pork. No malice intended.

By the way, how did St. Francis travel? He travelled in a small wooden canoe powered by his two hands around the world according to his brother in the Society of Jesus, the late Fr. Hudson Mitchel in one of our retreats.

Anyway, if it was enough for many simple early Christians - of whom many had no vision of Christ, to be singing in Circus Maximus in Rome while they were being eaten by hungry lions, what would that make of us spiritually? Nothing but a bunch of *self-seeking spiritual mediocre, would we not be?*

This idea of having achieved a **self-fulfilled life** like many rich pensioners who spend ironically their seemingly empty life on golf courses and cruises should have opened their kindred souls into infinite possibilities of becoming holier.

Don't get me wrong. I have nothing against golf courses or cruises. I just want seniors like what I am trying to do - give themselves a time for soul-searching. So, to be specific what I mean is that "my heart is restless" at age 79 **pre-date** my "sense of fulfillment."

We should not say, "*I am who am.*" Why? That is the name of God given to Moses for all mankind, not only to know but to love and adore Him. When people, like philosopher Descartes say, "*I think; therefore, I am,*" that is tantamount to claiming to be like God. We should instead say in all humility, "*I am; therefore, I think.*"

While to St. Paul a "**restless heart**" might have started his global evangelization "to find rest" in Christ, I walked away from that challenge and found myself at age 79, though "self-fulfilled" (much credit to my wife) on material things but ironically I still thirst for spiritual graces. It is like when you give me 10 dollars, I want 20$ more...

Let me tell you a little what I know about my thirst. Often, I ask the question, "*Is there a better life than what I have just fulfilled?*" "*Yes, there is.*" the Lord seems to say, and continues, "*I am surprised with your question, Elmer.*"

This answer was not from an **echo** chamber in my "sick" mind because it surprised me why God asked me such question. Wait, it might not have passed your torpid mind as it did to my 'torpe' mind but some questions especially coming from God like this is so simple that *it upsets my own stupidity.*

Remember, what I just wrote that when the Apostles asked about their dwelling places, Jesus answered them not to worry for, "*I have prepared a Mansion for each one of you in heaven?" (Corinthians 2:9).* This is God promising a "Mansion," festooned with flowers whose colors you have not seen - as Don Bosco once commented.

This Mansion for each one of us is not just a promise from another politician from heaven but from our Lord who said in the 3rd Luminous mystery of the rosary quoted by the St. John Paul II, "*The kingdom of heaven dwells in you.*"

By the way, for the excitement I have for a new Mansion (if I make it by the grace of God) after I have achieved my earthly Mansion on earth, how can you not understand why I want "**to die soon?**" Is it selfish for me to leave my loved ones and go to the other side? Far from it!

I recall St. Imelda Lambertini who loved God so much that she wanted to abandon herself and enter the convent at age 12. She kept begging to enter the convent like St. Therese, the Little Flower, until she was accepted.

Once in the convent she wanted to receive Holy Communion but was refused because one had to be 14 years old to receive Jesus – the norm at that time. With perfect obedience to her superior, she would just kneel for hours before the tabernacle, burning with great desire in her restless heart to be in *union with Christ even while on earth*. Is that beyond anyone to do? Tell me.

And one morning, Mother Superior saw her in a trance while receiving Holy Communion from the air. After receiving Communion, she lay on the floor and died. Truly, the late Bishop Sheen was right when he said, "*It does not take so much time to be a Saint; it only takes so much love.*"

To this day, the body of St. Imelda Lambertini lies incorrupt in Bologna, Italy. I knew this for a fact after I got married. And believe it or not, God in his divine providence, must have arranged her for me in the same way as He did for her.

When I saw her picture, it was the end of my bachelor life. God not wanting me to become a priest was a secret

I discovered beyond reasonable doubt when I married someone whose first name is the same as that of St. Imelda Lambertini.

So, every day with her, dull moments or happy ones during 43 years of our married life, has been a transforming opportunity for me to become a better man. Praise the Lord. Alleluia!

COMMERCIAL: Mother Angelica of the EWTN humorously speculated in one of her shows that they ran out of wine in the wedding feast of Cana a few hours after his twelve apostles arrived.

Indeed. Jesus could not refuse the **woman** (*Genesis, 3:15*) who gave birth to Him in Bethlehem. Even to this day, our Mother Mary continues to answer our prayers. I, then, believed where doubt apparently did exist: praying the rosary "*is the most powerful weapon (ref: Padre Pio) against the snares of Satan who prowls like a serpent, day and night seeking the ruin of souls.*"

From that day on, I started reciting my rosary more sincerely than just mumbling it as a mere *spiritual routine my earthly mother, Maria, taught me since I was a toddler.* NOTE: Do you want to know what sin Mother Mary stopped me short from doing so? If you know what sin by which Adam and Eve brought death to all generations so that we need a **second childbirth**, then I might tell you.

So, when someone wants to die soon like me, look at his life and you will know where he will go. If a man is going to Heaven, it is almost always **through the intercession** *of Mama Mary* that the grace of God is bestowed. If a man is going to Hell (God forbid) it is only a decision, he freely and willingly makes for himself.

Though God in his infinite love and mercy allows us to go to Hell, He never wills anyone to go to Hell. Hell is the arrogance of our "*pro-choice.*" Hell was not created by God but by the Prince of Darkness who reserves his dark place for his "beloved" friends on earth.

When Editor Elnora Minoza from Denver Colorado wrote to me, "*Elmer, we are now in the pre-departure area,*" it gives me a glimmer of humor rather than a morbid thought. Imagine, a plane as your coffin landing literally on my earthly "Mansion?" What better metaphor?

Yet, don't get me wrong. Desiring **"to die soon"** does not mean I am not fearful to think of dying. I am fearful. Very fearful. Perhaps more fearful than you are. It also does not mean to create a vain impression on your mind that I am a "Macho." I am not. I have never been, in case you sometimes inadvertently consider that for yourself.

To repeat, I am fearful of dying soon. Imagine, I have to leave a beautiful and wonderful wife, children that amuse me, nephews and nieces that adore me not because I am "loaded" but because of what I am to them as what they are to me. Matchochita? Maybe. Just kidding.

You cannot imagine the anxiety I cause my dearest wife whenever I mention the idea of dying even in a passing, humorous way. Though I know that I may cause such anxiety to my loved ones, the mystery of love that awaits one at the other side is hard to explain. It often bares me out to the **naked truth who did it for me in the 10ᵗʰ station of the Cross**. He was 33 years old. And man, I am a dry 79 years old and complaining?

Let me explain it this way: So why do I want "***to die soon?***" It is in order that **my free will** would be in **UNION with God's will**. For on earth, though in a modest way, I am trying to think like Christ, love like Christ and act like Christ, my poor heart wishes to die on St. Joseph's feast day, I have not become whole as I would by God's grace. At this juncture, pray for me.

Our heart is not like a **perfect valentine heart** we want. For we do not have a perfect heart to love. Every Valentine's Day we give our heart as perfect as we think. But look at your heart, a piece is missing on the left side (refer to Gray's anatomy).

Our Ven. Bishop Fulton Sheen said, "*God keeps a piece of it in Heaven,*" You have to die to yourself in order to retrieve and make your heart as perfect as a Valentine Heart as you enter the golden gate of Heaven. Amazing, is it not? But the metaphor is true.

I think that when my free will dies in *UNION with God's will*, I will experience through God's providence the essence of "**divine love.**" Divine love casts out fear and actually makes dying a perfect celebration to a world that is no longer just a temporary dream. We constantly pray everyday to our Mother in Heaven "*Pray for us sinners now and at the hour of our death. Amen.*"

So, who would not long for such a celebration when one is already out of this world, having fulfilled what God has commanded him to do? No more tears to wipe. No more death to mourn – *for such World, we often dread out of our own weaknesses, has passed away.*

I do not encourage you "**to die soon**" unless the cup of God's mission for you is **full of grace to the brim.** There is only one key to enter the golden gate of Heaven and enjoy your Mansion: "*Love God above all things and love your neighbor as you love yourself.*"

Do not fool around. Get that right. No one deserves to be in Hell, a place where people **have lost their goodwill while on earth.** In case you do not believe, although you are not to see its work, St. Padre Pio was not bothered about it when asked the same question. He answered with a smile, "*You will believe in Hell once you will be there.*"

❋

INSIDE THE NOTRE DAME CHURCH

Last May 8, 2015, around 9 A.M. inside the Notre Dame Church in Ogdensburg, New York, after praying at the 9th station of the Cross and I was on my way to the 10th I almost bumped an old Sister.

She was about 5'8" in height. I did not know: she was a Saint. I thought: she was just an ordinary Sr. who happened to pass by.

She was wearing a brown Franciscan habit with her hood covering her head. With my remaining tunnel vision, I had never seen such very beautiful blue eyes, smiling at me. She must be in her 80's but she looked a lot younger than her age.

As I stepped aside she touched my left shoulder as if like a mother to comfort a child, spoke a few words. Unfortunately, I could not understand what she was saying because I was not wearing my hearing aid.

As she passed by she walked with measured step as most seniors do (me included). She appeared heavy with her Franciscan habit like Mo. Angelica's weight and stature of the EWTN before her retirement from her TV show.

As she was gone behind the door I was wondering how she could manage to go down the 13 steps of the Notre Dame Church. Then, I proceeded to the 10th station.

Since I could hardly read 12 font due to Glaucoma I just simply talked before each station (and later I discovered that I could connect closer to Jesus), a lot better than simply reading a prayer book.

At the 10th station I felt deeply hurt to see Jesus standing naked before a mocking crowd, even the wind which was supposed to comfort him was carrying pain upon his open bleeding wounds. The picture was grotesque.

However, when I remembered what Fr. Gobi wrote that his own Mother gave up her white veil to cover his private part I felt relieved from the shameless crowd mocking at Him.

So, I thought: "If I will be judged by my sins after the resurrection of 'my' body" I have no chance for a happy "life everlasting. Amen."

Our Credo was clear when our Lord said, "I will judge the living and the dead." Hence, I wondered what wisdom could come out from Heaven to save all mankind.

Did not Christ come down from his Kingdom perhaps, a less populated Heaven in contrast to over populated Hell and appeared on earth on Jan. 2, 1931 to St. Faustina to announce his prayer of Divine Mercy at the very hour he died? Hence, I could only say, "Jesus, I trust in thee."

A couple of weeks passed by and while I was praying my rosary alone after the 6:45 AM Mass, this woman in Franciscan habit came slowly from behind me.

I was astounded. I never thought I would see her again for a life time, even in the remotest part of my brain's shallow niche.

She came nearer to me and gently touched my left shoulder as if like a Mother to comfort an 'old' child. She uttered a few words which perhaps were consoling words. But I could not hear. Again, I was not wearing my hearing aid.

She extended her left hand to me. And out of respect and reverence I kissed her hand. And suddenly I felt emotional and I became teary. I spoke trembling. "Please pray for me, Sister."

No doubt on my mind she must be a holy sister, living somewhere in our community. But I had never seen her for 21 years during Sunday Mass or daily in the small chapel of this church. Anyway, in case I might see her again, I now faithfully wore my hearing aid.

Four months had passed. I did not see her again. I decided to tell my spiritual confessor, Fr. James Shurtleff just in case he might have seen her. Or have known her. In the confessional box before confessing my sins I told him. It seemed he had not seen her and he suggested she might be a "Sister."

Weeks later after I saw the picture of stigmatist, St. Catherine of Siena, which was bugging my mind: it appeared to me she was the one.

Sr. Mary Siena Bracero of the Society of Angel of Peace seemed to concur. Someday, when I will be at the other side I would know her for sure, assuming I would be worthy at her sight.

I BELIEVE IN GOD'S
DIVINE MERCY

In less than an hour, I did not know that I could be dying, "Hour of Divine Mercy." It was Thursday, passed two o'clock in the afternoon, July 5, 2012. After 4 successive bouts of bloody stool at home, I had a strong feeling to go to the hospital.

After my wife saw about 150 cc of blood in the toilet bowl, she sadly agreed. She kept her cool. It was sunny when we walked in a hurry, across the street. After passing the Notre Dame Church, we arrived at the ER of the Claxon-Hepburn Hospital, some two minutes away.

Strangely, I felt at peace: no fear, pain or anxiety what the next moment would bring. My stamina for life had not left me. On the examining table, while taking my medical history, the ER physician did a rectal exam, unfortunately with my permission.

With my internal hemorrhoid guarding behind my rectal passage, it was kind of rough and painful, that I jolted out a bit. Who would not with his big Caucasian extra size index finger, pushed deep into the recesses of my Asian butt? Then, after withdrawing his bloody finger, he said aloud,

"This is Diverticulitis, most common" (at my age, 74). I thought there might have been some <u>excessive loss of mucosal surface</u>, most common at the sigmoid colon where massive pressure was needed to *"release feces into the rectum,"* and in this process, mucosal capillaries could easily break, issuing bright red blood, turning hard feces into tarry stool (*J. Spivak, M.C.P.I.M., 3rd Ed, p.261-262*).

Given a history of taking a total of aspirin 375 mg for 7 days due to my bad back, a history of small gastric ulcer by Endoscopy two years ago associated with tarry stool and too much to drink recently, July 4th, I could not rule out that the bleeding might have come from this gastric ulcer. Confident what I knew of myself, I proudly demanded an endoscopy first. It could not be *Diverticulitis*!

After the rectal exam, I carefully went down from the examining table. Feeling an urge, I felt that I had to go again. I sat on a bedpan nearby. And just on time a huge amount of bloody stool came out pouring one after another and filled the room with unbelievable odor of "sanctity."

After this episode, I tried to stand up Spartan like but my knees buckled underneath. And I was trying to reach for the wall to hang on my vision got blurry and like an old raging partially blind and deaf old bull who got hit by a young Troubadour's spear, I collapsed.

My wife and other ER personnel rushed to help me before my head hit the floor, and lifted me up back on the examining table. It was around three o'clock (the *hour of Divine Mercy* that I often would recite every 3 am and every 3 pm for years).

There was panic everywhere. While I was losing strength not necessarily consciousness, I signaled for a bedpan and huge amount of a watery warm soft stool came one after another (which Imelda and the ER Doctor estimated an acute blood loss of 250 cc).

And suddenly my entire body became limp. No more energy. I could not move or see. I blackout, leaving my right ear still working. I heard two units of blood were being infused and I said to myself, "*This hospital has a great ER staff.*"

In the inscape of my being, a strange awareness enveloped me (maybe, prayers from my love ones) and I was witnessing, perhaps hallucinating, what looked like an opaque disk in front, my brain, but within me, apparently, the details of my brain seemed going in disarray.

My wife whispered, "*How are you doing?*" with my dying voice, I said, "*I am holding on my brain,*" whose contents seemed going into oblivion. "*In preparation for what?*" I humbly queried. My hour of death like the hour of my Lord on the cross had at last come to me with a peaceful and resigned heart to God's will.

I knew that I was dying, and sang this ancient line from a far distant poet, "*Even the dying crimson light in the West and dark plutonian cloud hovers over me.*" Yet, the <u>peace of Christ</u>, which the world could not take away sustained me (*John 14:27*).

Our Lord did not abandon me in this hour to the Hades **(Acts of the Apostles 2:29-32)** and who by his death on the Cross had forgiven me of my own corruptions. The fear of death as we often view life at end, such as <u>anxiety, anger, a sense of hopelessness, and despair, (Satan's weapons of mass destructions for souls)</u> were beyond me through no merit of my own.

While everybody around me, doctor, nurses, Imelda were panicky, setting up double IVs, left and right arms, running fluid fast enough to bring me out of this dilemma, I suddenly felt that it seemed I was <u>within the hand of God</u>, the Father, (who decided to create me out of nothing light years ago before I was even conceived in my mother's womb with my father's "love-help").

At this very moment, I discovered, how little I knew, after 74 years of my existence – <u>*God's mercy, love, and forgiveness*</u> (*St. Francis, Canticles of Creatures, V 1-2*). I was at a loss how to show my gratitude in spite of many broken promises in the past that my confessor once told me, "*When do you stop such sin of sensualities?*" After his blessing, he said, "*Pray for me.*"

Lives of Saints took a new meaning to me; rosaries were diamonds spoken to Mama Mary from my heart. And how I wished despite my sinfulness, Christ would make me thru his Mother Mary, one among His chosen ones on earth, at least a good person to start with. I got emotional from the depths. I groaned inside me. "*Nobody is perfect. But with God nothing is impossible. And God is available to those who ask,"* (Matthew 19:31) I thought.

No doubt, I realized – how little I know of His love for me (who himself is love that lights the whole Universe and continues to create the beauty of this world). I began to understand a little of his incomprehensible love. And I felt ashamed of my <u>self-serving self</u> all these many years, reminding me what he said, *"Deny yourself... come and follow me..." (Matthew 16:24).*

Whether He would open the door of the everlasting world and place me there or back into my own finite world, I wondered. I had no free will to guide me or decide where I wanted to go. I was just simply waiting, not for his judgment but hopefully for his *Divine Mercy.* I was ready for His will, not mine.

It must have been this *Hour of Divine Mercy* and prayers of my love ones I left behind that tilted the balance between the thinned onion-skin, which separates between these two worlds that I came into full awareness. I was back where I was... in the ICU with my wife beside.

With my wife's loving hands on me I felt and realized for the first time, after 41 years of marriage, how little I knew of her great love and unassuming devotion for poor me. I could not help it: I wept and thanked God, the Father, for his greatest gift for me, in this hour of my need.

Before lunch time I received the *body and blood of our Lord*, whose passion and death on the Cross for me had no doubt strengthened me in my suffering. Just as the presence of Mama Mary under the Cross had consoled Jesus (John 19: 25-30), the visit of Ms. Eleanor, Fr. James Shurtleff, and Boyet-Alona's vibrant family had brightened my darkened spirit.

The following day I was scheduled for endoscopy to rule out gastric bleeding. From the OR my heart rate dropped to 32/min. (N-65-70/min). The nurse informed me I had 2nd degree heart block, skipped beat, and an atrial fibrillation, one step nearer to ventricular fibrillation, and my life would be over. To control my sugar, I received intermittently a shot of insulin whenever my sugar reached 250 mg up. I tried to hang on.

In the morning, the medical specialist started me on Terbutaline and tried to convince me that I needed a pacemaker. He said, *"People with pacemaker live longer than those who do not."* I understood that people in my condition often die in sleep or during work out.

About 7 hours of taking Terbutaline, my heart rate got wild from 96/min to 120/min. It went to 140/min and the machine went blank and then returned to 120/min. Ironically, I felt as if I was jogging while in bed. I kept requesting the nurse for my urinal almost every two hours because I felt making my water every so often till I fell asleep from exhaustion.

The next morning, I felt my bladder full. This time I could not do it alone because I was tied with a network of monitoring gadgets: IV fluid, EKG machine, oxygen, BP apparatus, my feet connected to a wire that had a balloon that alternately massaged my hind legs for better blood circulation in order also to prevent blood clots, which might lead me to having a fatal stroke.

This beautiful nurse untied me and handed the urinal. So, while she was holding the urinal with her face at the wall, to avoid looking what I was doing I kept busy searching my guy down below.

Finally, I got hold of this guy after a long awful moment of searching and done with: one liter of yellowish urine. To break that awful embarrassing long moment of her waiting, I offered my limp excuse and said, "*Sorry Miss, it took a little longer searching for my little…*" And together, we had a good laugh in spite of.

The schedule for colonoscopy was deferred because the Anesthesiologist and the Surgeon were not comfortable to perform the colonoscopy with my low heart rate without a pacemaker. So, the following day a pacemaker was attached under the skin above my heart. In the evening the next day, colonoscopy was performed.

Finally, after 6 days of hospitalization I was discharged. My wife, Imelda, was happy that the Endoscopy was negative; no bleeding ulcer. The pacemaker was smoothly doing well to control the fluctuating heart rate, and the colonoscopy's result confirmed that the ER Doctor's diagnosis of *Diverticulitis* without evidence of perforation was correct. He was right. I was wrong. May he forgive me of my arrogance. I have a new life to start with as a good person. So, help me, God.

❀

A PLACE APART

When you think of a place
Apart from Cebu, think of Argao.
In Cansuje's hinterland,
Where we once lived, we thrived
On Tikling and Camoting kahoy.

From Cansuje's horizon, standing
On Tanawa-an's hill is seen
San Miguel's tower where from its dome,
Rang once a huge Spanish bell to call
Its faithful for Mass at early morn.

Argao's streets bear the names
Of local heroes,
In Media, our house is a ghost now,
Humbled by the passing
Of persons, things from time-past.

Today, in Barangay Lamacan
The St. Michael's Monastery
Stands over neighborhood
Where within its heart, Sisters
of "The Society of Angel of Peace."

Founded by my Apo
Are heard singing praise to God,
Every dawn and sunset
In this Monastery, a Holy Place,
Probably apart from you.

Prologue: When you think of a place apart from Cebu City, 68 km. away going southeast, on a narrow but asphalted road, think of Argao. Argao is a first class and the largest municipality in the Province of Cebu, composed of 45 Barangays and complete with High School and College education.

This town had produced many notable persons. To mention a few, we have the former Chief of the Supreme Court, Hilario Davide, Jr., Sec. of Education, Narciso Albarracin, a bar topnotch, and the late Judge Cesar Kintanar. *(Internet, census 2010).*

So far, no movie houses yet. It has several decent restaurants, a beautiful beach resort along its white shoreline, a Motel for dignitaries and tourists alike. Zero crime rate. There are retired foreigners from Germany and other countries. Population: about 68,000 people *(census, 2012).*

Monologue: Let me start my life as a child growing up during World War II in Barangay Cansuje where forest and hills are located. In the enclave of Cansuje we lived and thrived there on rice and corn grains, supplemented with tikling and Camoting kahoy.

Barangay Cansuje is 18 km. from Argao poblacion. So, the gun battle between invading Japs and Filipino soldiers were confined in the neighboring Barangays of Argao poblacion.

However, outnumbered and outgunned often our Filipino soldiers would retreat into the mountainous part of Cansuje to re-group. The dead soldiers were buried with honors; the cowards surrendered with two hands off and some became Japs' informers. *(Later, most informers paid their life in the hands of the Guerrilla Unit, some led by Mr. Pastor Abear)*.

Those who retreated into the mountains became known as Guerrilla Unit. Like Nong Pastor Abear and his comrades they regrouped and trained themselves for further covert action at night against the occupiers, the Japs. *(NOTE: Capt. Pastor Abear was a Purple Awardee for bravery of the Philippine Army for a successful defense of his unit during an ambush staged by anti-government forces in the 50's)*.

The Japs stayed in Argao, made the school, which was fronted by Acacia trees, their garrison. But one night they saw a Kapre smoking on branches of these huge Acacia trees by the moonlight and they fled in fear. The Kapre did a better job than the Guerrilla unit. If you don't believe about Kapre, ask some seniors in Argao - who are now in their 90's. Hurry, there are not enough of them left. Remember, faith is more than reason.

It was rumored, as a matter of fact, that Capt. Villamor from Argao, not the pilot, with about 250 elite Philippine Scouts volunteered for Gen. Douglas McArthur, Pres. Manuel Quezon, Carlos Romulo, and staff members to escape from Bataan to Manila bay where a submarine was waiting for them.

In the skirmishes that followed on their way out to escape most if not all - of about 250 elite Philippine Scouts who held their ground perished. Gen. McArthur was so impressed with their gallantry that he shouted his famous line, "*I shall return!*"

Meanwhile, Cansuje because of its distance from Argao center was beyond the reach of the Japs. In the enclave of Cansuje, we lived in peace and thrived on camoting kahoy, with chicken (left over by Banug and Oyak) and kamongay once a month.

One night while all of us, 5 kids, were eating our share of chicken and kamongay, Brod Jess who had the biggest share did not touch his. He wanted to be the last to eat so we would be enviously looking at him.

When we were almost done, Brod Jess began to finger his share and discovered that what was inside the kamongay was not chicken's leg he expected, but a fat rat instead. We could not help but laughed and Brod Jess showed his canine teeth, mad at us. I guessed that he "missed" the rat that night.

My Papa and Brod Cesar built a spring 150 feet below our bamboo-nipa hut in Cansuje while Brod Johnnie combed the muddy paddies getting ready for planting the rice seedling. Almost every morning Brod Johnnie would bring 2-3 Tiklings he got from his trap in the rice field the night previous.

Unfortunately, one afternoon while Brod Lading and I and some kids were playing, "*tubig-tubig*" a huge black dog of our neighbor across our house below came and bit Brod Lading's right arm badly.

A man rushed Brod Lading to our house up on a hill. They tried to control the bleeding and applied *ahos* (ginger ale). And I heard Brod lading shouted with great pain. I guessed, the *ahos* was more painful than the dog's bite. This treatment was done to prevent Brod Lading from getting rabid if in fact the dog was rabid. To this day Brod Lading has not been acting like a mad dog. The *ahos* was certainly working.

Meanwhile, I saw Nong Tito Minoza chased the dog with a piece of wood. The dog ran across the rice paddies and up on the hill and Nong Tito followed. Finally, the dog returned home. And there on the porch of the house Nong Tito beat his head to death while the owners were looking and could not do anything.

In the Minoza's residence not far from our bamboo-nipa house, across rice paddies, Brod Lading and I went there frequently to play with cousins Eddie and Baby May, hide and seek, laughing and getting lost in between sunflowers across their front yard. Today, I could still remember the scent of sunflowers and dandelions. Thanks to God, my nose has been better than my memories.

Oh, how I loved Cansuje during the day. If I was not playing *tubig tubig* I went chasing Tikling on rice paddies until my legs got heavier with suckers (alimatok). But I hated Cansuje when the night came: there were witches to worry about. They scratched the wall, "caskas" the roof and made weird sounds.

My older brothers said: they were witches from Naga looking for kids who refused to sleep. *(NOTE: I found out later that these witches were my brothers like Ondo and Ernesto. I was not surprised: they looked like witches to me anyway.)*

If you walk from Cansuje on your way to Argao poblacion, you will climb a mountain called Tan-awan beside Lantoy, and you will have a good view through a misty distance of about 16 kilometers away, the dome of San Miguel's tower.

Once a 100-year-old huge Spanish bell inside the dome of this tower would twang bang to awaken the faithful to attend Jesus' early Mass. Now, the sound of the bell could be heard no more. However, the short hand and the long hand of the giant clock outside had stopped, unmoved surely by the absence perhaps of the huge bell. I wonder if that century's bell is still there.

Our house was located not far from the market place called Media. I vividly remember what Mama told me about a group of advanced seniors who would be knocking at our house one night around four in the morning on their way to attend Mass at San Miguel Church.

They were being chased by dwarfs. My Papa drove those little creatures of God back to where they belonged - to the chimneys in the market place. If you don't believe in dwarfs, I don't blame you. Mama might tell some white lies but since Papa confirmed this story, I do believe. A person who read the Holy Bible every dawn like my

Papa, in my opinion, could not tell lies. He read the bible, Thomas e Kempis, Thomas Merton down to his last days in life.

Along Media street our house is still standing there like a ghost, humbled but evoking memories about the passing of things and persons of time's past. When there was literally peace overseen, and maintained by the Japs for almost three years in Argao poblacion, we sometimes went down from Cansuje to Argao proper.

Brod Lading and I could not go to Argao poblacion with Papa unless we carried two gantas of corn on our head. For an eight year old it was really heavy on my head. Nevertheless, I had to carry it with a heavy heart. Argao poblacion was just exciting to miss.

When I reached Argao after 5 hours' walk, I felt shorter by one inch. So, I had to stretch my head every morning to regain my height. Brod Lading did not do such, so he was shorter by one inch. I loved to see the hairy calvarium of his head, heh, heh.

I still remember one afternoon around three o'clock when two Filipinos who became Japs' comrades in arms came to our house in Barangay Lamacan, asking for a glass of water, leaving their two captured suspected Guerillas who were brothers on the road, with hands tied.

While the Japs' comrades were drinking water the two brothers were able to untie themselves and ran as fast as they could. One of the comrades immediately went to the road, aimed and shot the brothers: one was hit and fell on the creek; the other was able to escape running into the sugar cane field.

When Papa heard the shot while he was in the sugar mill building he ran towards the house. When the Japs' comrade saw him running he knelt down to take a shot at him. Then, I heard Nang Mary, wife of Emelio, shouting repeatedly at the top of her voice,

"Don't shoot! He is my father! Don't shoot! He is my father!" And the Japs' comrade heard her pleading and he did not. Nang Mary, no doubt, clearly saved the life of my father.

Immediately, I saw blood in the water flowing from the small creek in front of our house from the wounded alleged Guerrilla. I could hear the man was groaning with pain. The Jap comrade went into our house and demanded that one of my brothers should go down to bury the wounded Guerrilla alive. Or else he threatened to execute all of us. Brod Emelio, Alfredo, and Johnnie were hiding in the chimney.

When Brod Johnnie heard that all of us would be killed he went down from the chimney to do the job. The Japs' comrade had already tied both feet and hands of the alleged wounded Guerrilla. With Brod Johnnie on one end of the bamboo they carried him like a dead pig about to be roasted and placed inside the Tartanilla of our neighbor.

Brod Johnnie slowly drove away to the cemetery, some 4 kilometers away. While he was away we all gathered, and prayed on our knees the rosary before our Lady asking for his safe return. After hours of agonizing and anxiously waiting for him, he at last, arrived home safe.

He said, that when he was midway to the cemetery the man stopped groaning and died. The horse perhaps in respect of the dead refused to pull the Tartanilla no matter what maneuver he did. So, he had to be the "horse" to pull the Tartanilla. After agonizing hours, he finally reached the cemetery and buried him. Brod Johnnie, no doubt, had saved us from being executed.

In Barangay Lamacan where this incident took place, not far from our residence, was Papa's mini sugar mill.

He supplied the staple in the area. The Japs used to pick up their supply in the morning while the Guerilla unit picked up theirs late in the evening. We prayed the Rosary twice, day and night, so that they would not encounter. Prayer worked. They did not have an encounter.

Praying the rosary (plus novenas) was one of the most boring hour for small kid like me. But if I did not pray or sleep in between prayers I got my ears wound up, clockwise. It was a relief later when it was clear that there was no encounter between the Guerrillas and the Japs: our rosary time was reduced to once a day at night time. I used to sleep ahead of prayer time. Sleeping was not boring, zzzzz…

Whenever a Jap medic came and painted my boils red with "Micro chrome" I had to cover my left eye because my brothers warned me that the Japs would adopt me if they found out about my left eye. Why? They said that I would be a "Wonder Jap" with only one slit eye while the Japs had or have two slit eyes (No insult intended).

Then in 1946 Gen. McArthur made his promise. His G.I. (short for "Ground Infantry" of the U.S. Army) arrived in Argao via Leyte. It was rumored that when McArthur landed in Leyte he could not find Carlos Romulo.

It was allegedly said when Gen. McArthur lifted a floating helmet beside him, presto! It was Romulo, smiling, as if saying, "*Please, don't make waves, Sir.*" There was not enough gun battle between the G.I. and the Japs in Leyte and in Argao because the Japs knew beforehand of their arrival and preferred to run away.

At this point, Baby May passed Nang Aurora Minoza's song of welcome to me when Gen. McArthur returned:

When the lights of hope are fading
for the peace, we long have craved.
Fix your thoughts upon their promise,
"I shall return."

Don't forget we have our Savior,
Led by Gen. McArthur
Who bravely planned,
"I shall return."

Filipinos stand by him,
Peace and hope will help us win.
I shall return sings loud and clear...

You are at last in our shores!
Rejoice! Thank God!

We shall be free that means
Will have liberty…
Keep it clear in every heart…
HE HAS RETURNED!

(NOTE: Miss Aurora A. Minoza, graduated from U.P. Diliman, Magna Cum Laude. Under Fulbright Smithmundi Scholarship she completed her Masters at the Michigan State University, U.S.A. became President Foundation University, Dumaguete City, Southern Philippines).

In our 7-room residence in Media, the G.I. found a home away from home for them to stay in, courtesy of Argao's acting Mayor, who was appointed by Gov. Cabahug, and sworn into office by Lieutenant Smith. I remember that after dinner the G.I.'s gave Papa some tip but Papa would politely refuse. Later, we discovered they put their dollars under the plates.

Anyway, where was the incumbent Mayor Pena? Some Guerrilla unit allegedly killed him for being suspected of collaboration with the Japs during its occupation. Nevertheless, the good heart of the Argawanon still honors him as one among the local heroes who served the town well. His photo seen in the municipal building today is a testimonial.

At night, I still remember, Brod Lading and I would ransack ration No. 2 that the G.I. kept under the house for distribution to the poor people. We were searching for a *Butterfly* chocolate and peanuts. If we asked, we got only one or two pieces of chocolates, so stealing was a good business.

Yet, in one out of five forays, we were caught. A whistle blower I could not rule out. Indeed, we got whacks on our butts, a sin more "enjoyable dancing" than munching a butterfly nut and cookies. Could you imagine what he used to whack us with?

A private part of the cow tied with a stone and suspended up on a coconut tree so it would stretch longer than what short a private part it was. It hanged like a pendulum in the wind and made to dry for a week enough to harden what soft a private part it was, hard enough like a police "batota."

Who would not dance, jail house rock, when hit by this "batota?" I loved the discipline: it made me smarter like Robin Hood at night time. After all, one out of five that we were caught red handed was not bad a statistic. The consequence of sin, that was the "batota", was something I could take in favor of munching chocolates. Mama called me, "*hard headed.*" Mama was wrong because it was my butt that was hard of callus.

I recently visited Cansuje with the late Nene Molina and still noticed my Papa's spring which he built with Brod Cesar. It still flows into the rice field like graces from heaven. On top where our nipa hut was once located, it was now vacant save for some tobacco and kamoting kahoy planted, evoking a reminiscent of things and persons of time's past.

Further from this place toward south was a small kalasangan. To go there one would climb a small steep hill about 200 feet high and beyond was the Kalasangan. I remember there was a small clearing up on a hill.

On that clearing I saw a group of young women who were working under the heat of the sun. One with a large sombrero, wearing long sleeves stopped and glanced at me: it was cousin Leonie Minoza holding a bolo.

Cousin Leonie smiled at me: she was a beautiful woman. Then, she continued planting Camote. *(Later, she entered the Missionary Sisters after graduating from Pharmacy at the University of the Philippines in the 50's. She is still in the convent at age 90, happy and healthy in my recent contact by e-mail).*

Epilogue: Today, in Barangay Lamakan, along Lamakan's unpaved road, not far from the sea coast on a small hill, stands the beautiful Monastery of St. Michael, home of the Sisters of *"The Society of Angel of Peace,"* a congregation (I did not know) founded by my Apo.

The Monastery stands magnificent and awesome, perhaps, a reflection of things and persons of time's past. From the heart of this *"St. Michael's Monastery"*, from sun down to sun up, you can hear the beautiful singing of the Sisters, giving praise and thanks to our Lord, Jesus Christ, for his gift and the beauty and peace of this town, a place apparently apart from you.

A BLACK LIFE MATTERS

Three black robbers were shot dead in the street of New York, some years ago, with what seemed a failed Bank heist. One of them chronicled to the media that he saw his body lying dead in the street.

The next moment, he was in darkness and smelled a bad odor, nothing like it on earth. From a distant he saw a huge burning pot spewing fire up into the air. He was slowly moving toward the burning pot.

Even if he wanted to stop and stay away from it, he could not: he had lost his freedom of choice. Slowly, he was moving: it seemed by the will of Someone he did not know or understand.

He saw his 2 buddies fell into the burning pot as he was getting closer. The scenery was horrible. Again, nothing like it on earth, it must be a place called Hell. He apparently did not believe in Hell but now that he saw it, he believed.

As he was about to fall into the burning pot, contrite from his heart for the first time, he shouted, "Jesus Christ!" Name he used on earth whenever he cursed. Immediately he was dangling, holding on the rim of the pot, and he heard his two buddies shouting, "Hold on! If you fall you will never return."

He woke up in the morgue ready for autopsy. The Mortician was amazed and said, "He is alive!" The ER Doctor who pronounced him dead rushed and brought him to the intensive care unit and resuscitated him back to his earthly life.

After a week, he was discharged in good spirit. He went to jail for the crime he committed. For the greater glory of God, he became a Minister for lost souls. Alleluia!

✻

A SENSE OF DESPAIR
AND THEN, NOTHINGNESS

To begin with, a sense of loss is defined here as a precursor of a **contrive**, Greek word, "diabolus," which means a diabolical feeling of <u>self-indulgence</u> that often breaks what is beautiful of self and to what is ugly before the eyes of God and before our love ones...

From Rossana's diary, she wrote: "*You have everything and yet you have nothing.*" How many people, rich and poor (ratio 10:1) when overcome with a sense of loss take away their life? In the finality of life, our Lord warned: "*What does it profit a man if he gains the whole world and at the end suffers the loss of his own soul?*"

One great man in history had truly understood that. With losing everything worldly, what he planned for himself was to go around the world in a small canoe and "set the world on fire" for Christ. This man is the incorrupt St. Francis Xavier, S.J.

Yet, today as what the Word of God has predicted, our ugliness is manifested in the form of human being. What better definition is it for me to hear one night over the National TV a young beautiful woman proclaimed (to justify abortion), "*I own my body.*" Whenever we have lost **shame** we have lost the **grace** of life, and hence the **culture of death** begins to dominate our life.

Yet, as some of us survive this kind of <u>self-centeredness</u> we search for hope. Hope to overcome our sense of loss. Our sense of hopelessness. Of nothingness. In the struggle between good and evil within ourselves Socrates once wrote: "*An unexamined self is not worth living.*"

As we begin to examine the good that is within us, we cannot help but encounter a person bigger than ourselves. This requires humility, which gracefully melts down any form of our falsehood, and open up ourselves to a higher being we call, **God**, **Almighty**. If you cannot accept this end result of all searching, I think, there is no need to read this dissertation any further. You waste your time. But definitely, not mine.

If you read further out of that ancient feeling of curiosity, let us start by saying, *God is our only hope*. Because He alone and no other, can draw beauty out of our own ugliness just as he did (and many others in history) to a prostitute, St. Mary Magdalene. God did not come for the good but for the sinners, who needed redemption.

Many pseudo intellectuals, now and in the past, (to mention one, the author of this blasphemous book, The Da Vince Code) have defiled this love of God for the forsaken people, who have lost hope, by disguising as fiction trumped with facts. What can one gain by not respecting the sacred beliefs of others, regardless of what faith they belong to?

The answer is: Nothing. One gains nothing except a sense of nothingness, a reflection of people whose souls like demons, *are seeking the ruin of souls* in a 24-hour basis. Yet, God as our only hope can **call us to holiness** anytime and by his grace we can be transformed as his little children of Mary, the Mother of God. You know, believe the incredible and God will make it possible.

A man who was once God's ***image and likeness*** (beauty as such) was lost in sin. The sin of disobedience (after Adam) has run deep in our 12 factors of blood like the 12 apostles, ever since. And only God's love on the Cross could wash away the sin and restore mankind into the splendor of his own image and likeness. Hence, our Lord said, "*Without me, you can do nothing.*"

It took me years of good and bad experiences to understand the lesson in between my gray matters that "Without *God, I am indeed nothing.*" Before his **Word**, I realized all my falsehood in life gracefully melts away, leaving me naked before him who created me.

And so, it is with you. If you allow him the way you allow sunlight to enter your dark room by opening a window, you will begin to see the light of the world. Remember, though how much God loves you, it is always you who must open the window. As our Lord said, "*Knock and you shall be opened.*" This time, you literally knock at your own window so a streak of sunlight can enter your dark room.

For a break, let me read to you this simple nugget whenever "doubt" like Thomas enters your heart and mind as it does with me sometimes: Try to see the insight of this unfinished poem and like Thomas touch the wound of the unlimited reality of God:

Flower and Eagle invite me
Into the brink of nothingness,

Where doubt distresses me
Until I hear in my wounded self
The Word of a dying God.

I am eager
Like a morning bee upon a flower
To know that grace is not fleeting.

I am eager
Like an eagle with strong wings
To know that the blue sky is for real.

And to let me understand the night
When the evening comes with its stars.

If you don't see the depth of the sky, the mystery of grace that often eludes us our desire, this poem is lost into nothingness. We came from nothing, remember? God breathed into the earth and Adam blossomed. Let us forget for a while what happened to the red apple. Let us focus and remember we came from nothing. If we believed that, faith of the eagle alone suffices the understanding of the evening stars.

Faith in God seems to cut through the devilish details of our own life and often lay bare the essence of the mystery of our own existence. If we do not grasp that, let the sky over our head suffices. Even the devil could not explain us out. Our mind has his own free will; its own evil and goodness that needs no other help before it is sealed forever after death. Understand?

If you do not understand you are lucky. Why? There is hope. On the Cross, there is forgiveness to those who do not know. "*Father, forgive them for they do not know what they are doing.*" Is ignorance an excuse for not falling into hell? Can presumption be a good principle of life?

However, in my opinion, ignorance is not a ticket to heaven. To go to heaven, you must be perfect. A little glass you might be, but certainly *full* to the brim of God's love and grace. No one enters the gate of heaven who is not perfect. That is not my opinion. It is the Word of God to **man**, who according to Bishop Fulton J. Sheen, is *"God's hell."*

Do not forget that, we can go to hell without the help of the fallen angels who *prowl all over the world seeking the ruin of souls*. Yet, ironically we cannot go to heaven without God's amazing grace. Unfair to the devil, is not it? Our nothingness, out of which we came, could explain that difference. I hope.

Without God, therefore in our heart of hearts, who then could inhabit our heart? God is light and so without Him there is nothing but darkness. Darkness could dwell in our darkened heart. In the darkness of bitterness, anger, and hate we thirst for the light of joy and love if we want to survive in peace with ourselves.

Yet, for us to have light we humbly need God. For God is

light and with Him and in Him every unanswered desire of the heart or dream can find its rest. Provided we are not sold to darkness, to hopelessness, and to despair.

Therefore, *go gentle into the dark night*, to borrow Dylan Thomas' song, and be not outraged to ask – "*What personifies nothing anyway?*" The answer is: Nothing. Nothing could only be expressed its own diabolical ugliness. Ugliness that is forced upon us daily by the beauty we know, if and only if, we know of any. If you don't know anything "beautiful" in your miserable life you deserve to be exorcised.

Even though something grotesque he is crowned with the tinsel title entirely of his own making, The Prince of Darkness, is the devil. A devil means a "*split person.*" Whenever he talks he confuses you like a broken chair inviting your bum.

Whenever we are tempted, Mo. Angelica suggests that we say to the devil, "*You are nothing. Go away.*" And you know what? Mother Angelica's devil goes away.

That is why, in my opinion, Mo. Angelica is a living saint. I hope I have that kind of devil who goes away, heh, heh...

My devil, to some extend like me, does not have a soft head. As my own mother once said, "*Elmer, you're stubborn and worse, hard headed.*" *Testadora,* as Mo. Angelica's mother used to call her when she was small. If you know me, you have no option but to pray. If I happen to know you, well, God forbid...

By the way, what do you think of your devil? If you say that you don't have one, the odd is greater that you do not have because unfortunately you have become a demon, yourself (No offense intended). It is like when you do not believe in sin you call God a liar. Devil does not know himself. That is why. And that's part of the hell inside him. And to those of his own kind.

Sorry, if you feel I misjudged you. You pushed me into that kind of mentality. It's only a "broken" opinion, you might say. And you are right. Why? It's not your opinion. Do I beg my own question? I can feel the shallowness of my thought. It seems, I am leading you into the brink of my own "nothingness." It seems that I am lost. As Edgar Allan Poe, would say, "*Darkness there and nothing more.*"

Let us go forward to what more there is in life. Do you know that anything harmonious and beautiful would set Satan's adrenalin up? His ugliness could not stand it.

Just as darkness and light have nothing in common (save perhaps a gray line) there is nothing common between beauty and ugliness (save perhaps indifference). To which, I remember, our Lord said, "*I'll vomit you out of my mouth.*"

The devil goes around the world as an "omnipotent" being, preaching without words of pleasures - "*drink and be merry for tomorrow you die,*" and silently you can say to yourself, "*Be the kind of ashes of repentance I wear behind my brain during Lenten season.*"

St. Theresa, the little flower, was overcame with the idea, that *"there is nothing after death,"* as few of us do. This idea crushed her faith in what God said, that *"there is heaven after a good and holy life."* Though often we argue that "I do not exist between my sleep," sometimes a dream comes through, that we still do exist even in just a dream. Hence, dreamless night does not rule out your nonexistence.

However, St. Theresa held on tenaciously with prayer and so darkness left her. Because prayer itself is a kind of light that could cast the darkness aside. Surely, her faith was restored as she continued in the silence of the convent, *"Doing heaven on earth by doing good."* Can you believe by that principle of life she became a Doctor of the Church?

Allow that principle of life, *doing ordinary things in an extraordinary way*, (which Rossana silently did in her lifetime) by asking the grace of God. And surely, God will transform your life. Like St. Theresa, the Little Flower, you will find heaven on earth. If you don't believe this truth, as Bishop Fulton Sheen once said, the truth will still remain the truth just as when you believe a lie it still remains a lie.

A young, talented and lovely Tara Lipinski kissed the statue of St. Therese, the Little Flower in public and it earned her a Gold Medal in figure skating held in Nagano, Japan last 1998. How many of us saw and believed? Don't ask me. I am St. Theresa, the little flower's fan. Don't tell me about "coincidence" the devil's travesty to remove grace for doubt, then doubt to skepticism. What does it gain you? Again, *nothing*.

Looking back nowadays through three decades the work of this devil is manifesting everywhere. This is the voice of the minority – anything that resembles God be removed from schools, offices, flag, money, sadly even in some Churches – while the majority does nothing. So, *evil thrives because good people do nothing*.

In another setting, the idea of nothingness is presented often as something "pleasurable, attractive, and beautiful." Of course, who can resist it? That is why, he gets a lot of followers. This road that Satan promises is wide because it is where most people travel.

Hence, a holy man is convinced that his road is narrow and difficult so that few souls ever venture. (This theological analogy of course is subject to change when we talk about the pathway to sin and grace, read "Pathway to Heaven," *Life and Death, its humor and sorrows).*

When this dark spirit enters the heart of those looking after the Church for the last three decades, it leaves the Church empty. Beautiful paintings and statues which remind us of the beauty of the place where they were, walked out into the darkness of the night either with the consent of the caregivers or some robbers.

So much so, that even the dark hardwood kneelers in Argao left the Church. Most Catholic Churches like most Protestant Churches are empty now. They are empty like community halls where people talk and "pray." Satan works best in the "hour" of darkness.

God must have thought we need something like the World Trade Center to wake us up. Or Russian planes and submarine encroaching the freedom of our space to humble and ridicule us, as one poet would say, "An intimidation to immortality." We can paraphrase that to some Russian leaders, not its wonderful people, by saying, "An intimidation to destructibility." I am not saying that God loves to punish us.

Often, we just love to punish ourselves and God simply provide what we appropriately need to satisfy our dementia. If I am wrong, bear it with me. I only know winter is here when I hear no robins singing in the air and see naked trees like frightened fingers caught frozen in the wan wood night.

When this Prince of Darkness, which the Holy Bible mentioned would enter and set in holy places of the Churches would be over, peace would reign, an idea, it seems, beyond the threshold of hope. However, where the night is greatest in our age of moral melt down and decadence, the light is even more luminous like the way Pope John Paul II sees it, "*We are witnessing the coming of the springtime of Christianity,* a voice it seems from the wilderness as John the Baptist to the people during his time.

With the tribulations, we are experiencing nowadays, a chaotic weather that takes billions of our money, not to mention lives and properties, crime of the young and old, the almost daily casualties in Iraq and elsewhere, the preparation for world peace under the stock files of nuclear weapons, I guess, the justice of God when his mercy has ended not run out, would come as our Lord said, "*Like a thief in the middle of the night.*"

Then, we will begin to understand this when people start going to Churches and pray, when the statues of our crucified Jesus, our Virgin Mother and her Saints would come back in their right places in the Church for us to once again love and to venerate.

Once again, what we will see inside our Church is the beauty of our faith, not the emptiness and nothingness of Satan. It comes to us at a time when we are weary of vanity of vanities, when we begin to see the meaning and purpose of life. We then cease to become a terrorist to ourselves.

Therefore, the idea of nothingness is a place we no longer go, a place Christ once said, "*Where there is gnashing and grinding of teeth in the everlasting fire, the everlasting fire where "nothingness" forever dwells.*"

An idea of nothingness that has becomes forever "something." Indeed, nothing has become "something," that only man and Satan could figure it out of their own free will. God did not create hell; He simply allowed it to happen, out of the mystery of his love and mercy.

Whenever the feeling of nothingness comes to us, God understands that. In fact, he foresees its coming and allows it for own good to take place. But he admonishes us, because he loves us. He wants us to pray. Pray the

Rosary, our Mother's solution for world peace. Try if you have not used this strongest weapon against war and pestilence.

To those who do not pray, therefore what do we expect but the sense of hopelessness which is akin to a sense of nothingness. It is a vicious cycle, recycled within a perfect dark and hopeless pit, where as one poet wrote, *"Black is the pit from pit to pole."*

When our Lord saw the devil in Peter who disappointed Him so many times He warned him that the devil would use him like a "whip" but admonished him not to worry because *"I will pray for you, Peter." Can you imagine God in his human form praying for you? Can you imagine that we crucify him every time we commit a grievous sin? That is why, people in hell do not complain where they are. Neither those in heaven for their heart is full of overflowing joy.*

On a human level, that is what our Lord does to us. He loves us so much that every minute somewhere in the world, day and night, He offers Himself in the holy sacrifice of the Mass as the Lamb of God who takes away the sin of the world. And don't worry if you might fall into hell or do not make it to heaven, there is purgatory to clean your remaining mess.

Too often, we are good at comprehending the perfection of self, like most Buddhist do. Yet, this could be also the first step to seek the perfection of God in ourselves. Learn to unlearn yourself by knowing by heart what his eight beatitudes meant and thus follow his commandment, **"Thou shall love God above all things, above thy own self."**

Tired of Jesus praying to his heavenly Father deep into the night while the 12 apostles slept, Philip, one of His followers, asked our Lord pluperfect: "*Master, show us the Father!*" And said, our Lord looked at him and said: "*Philip you have been with me all these years and you do not know the Father. He who sees me, sees the Father, for the father and I are one.*"

Just as St. Augustine of Hippo could not understand what Jesus said to Philip, we too cannot understand this mystery. One God in three Divine Persons: The Father, the Son and the Holy Spirit. And so, like St. Augustine we could walk away from the seashore of our life towards God, accepting that God as a little child could indeed put the whole ocean in one small hole. Alleluia!

❈

MY UPPER DENTURE

This morning at 5 am, still dark, I went to the kitchen for a snack prior receiving communion at 7:15 am. On my way to the kitchen I passed by at the washroom to do my morning routine, emptying my basket and bag for today's bread from Heaven.

On my way out I picked my dentures, fitted the lower but on hold the upper one. At the kitchen, I quickly switched on the light so the bulbs got busted. It was dark for my glaucomatous eyes.

Anyway, I proceeded to grab the water heater in prep for my coffee while doing so my upper denture fell and I distinctly heard without a doubt in spite of not wearing my hearing aid.

I immediately sat down and groped with my hands and instead gathered the dirt I left last night: no denture found. I was surprised. I looked for a broom and cleaned up all corners till the floor was shiny bright. Which would surely surprise my partner in life, a humble task I often failed to do.

I thought of waking up my partner to help me locate my upper denture. But on the 2nd thought, experience wise, I cancelled it lest it might upset her and missed the shining floor.

I literally gave up and went to the kitchen table, some 4 feet away and boy, there on the table, my front denture looking at me, "Nag ngisi wara ug buhi."

❀

NOTE: If you don't believe in Guardian Angels, <u>you miss half of the fun in life</u>. Just try it. It worked with me over a hundred times over serious matters and minor silly ones, like my lost denture.

If you don't believe in miracle <u>you miss the remaining half of your life</u> in exchange for <u>Diabolus</u>, who is <u>nothing</u>. This is a bargain you cannot afford to lose. Got it? I named my Guardian Angel, Joel. What's yours?

"LORD, TEACH ME HOW TO PRAY"

The 12 Disciples who were simple fishermen, except Judas Iscariot, were appointed by Jesus Christ. Jesus knew that they *did not know how to pray*, perhaps unlike the white-bearded Pharisees who daily prayed in the Temple of King David.

Since we mention the word "Temple," let us recall the confrontation between the Pharisees and Jesus. Jesus said, "*Destroy this Temple and in 3 days I will raise it up.*" And the Pharisees said, "*It took 46 years to build up and in 3 days you will raise it up.*" *(Matthew 15:33-37).*

The same Pharisees in the person of Caiaphas, who was successful to arrest Jesus thru the help of Judas Iscariot asked this question that perhaps bothered him for years,

"*Are you the Son of God?*" And Jesus consistently said, "*Thou has said it.*" And Caiaphas tore his cloth from top to bottom and said, "*Thou hast blasphemed.*" Since he noticed Jesus was a good man, he said, "*It is better for one man to lose his life than our nation.*"

It is interesting to note: that when Jesus died on the Cross, the temple tore from top to bottom. An act, which only God can do. Usually we destroy the "Temple" from bottom up. As you may recall the break of the temple from top to bottom signaled a new era: the birth of Christianity as we see today.

Anyway, let us go back to where we left. Jesus facing his new disciples knew that <u>they did not know to pray</u>. So, Jesus told them, "*This is how to pray…Our Father who art in Heaven who art in Heaven hallowed be thy name thy kingdom come thy will be done on earth as it is in Heaven." (Luke 1: 2)*

Anyway, before we proceed any further let us meditate on the sentence: "*Thy Kingdom come thy will be done on earth as it is Heaven."* For years, I had routinely prayed the "Our Father" until recently I was amazed that the Kingdom of God, and that is Heaven, can also be down on earth for those who do the will of God.

The Kingdom of God, that is Heaven, must had been enjoyed by the living Saints in our midst namely, Padre Pio, St. John Paul II, Mo. Angelica of the EWTN, Ven. Bishop Fulton J. Sheen, to mention a few.

For them to enjoy Heaven on earth, they must had been what Jesus said, "Blessed are the poor in spirit for theirs is the Kingdom of God." Their being poor in spirit, is their humility, unlimited patience, and forgiving heart, must have allowed them to experience peace in their heart of hearts, amidst the trouble surrounding them.

Not only that they must had been amazed by the beauty of this world, as God the Father continues to create seeds that would fill the earth with fruits, beans, rice, corn etc. He would fill the sea with all kinds of fish to fry and animals like pigs and turkey esp. for Thanksgiving and beef for our barbecue. And dogs and cats to keep us in good company when our friends often fail.

Can you imagine God feeds us 3 times a day, some people 6 times a day, that they become obese? Hence, people who thank God, pray before and after meal. Do you?

During the day, God delights us faithfully with the sun that shines over all kinds of people, good or bad. No discrimination. And at night He fills the sky with stars and moon to make us curious what lays beyond the space we see. If this is not like Heaven on earth what else can it be? such as grow our food.

"Hail Mary full of grace..." was the salutation by the Angels to Mary, and apparently was repeated by Elizabeth when Mary visited her to help the delivery of John the Baptist. And whoever was the holy priest who completed it by adding, "*Holy Mary Mother of God pray for us sinners.*" I do not know. (Tradition as old *as the year 1030*).

In the beginning, it seemed St. Francis of Assisi did not know <u>how to pray.</u> St. Francis advocated the best prayer, which was not words (when words often fail), as an example. He said to his simple follower, "*Let us go down town and preach.*"

After going around town and returned home, his follower said, " I thought, we were to preach." St. Francis answered. "We have just preached by the brown habit we are wearing."

Honestly, I, myself, do not know <u>how to pray</u>, so I spend my time praying the Rosary every chance I get. Recently, it came to my mind that maybe I will wear the "Warrior Rosary" around my neck. The word "Warrior Rosary" is just fit for any brave Catholic to wear around his neck.

My intention of wearing a Rosary as my necklace is to try to popularize *how to pray the Rosary by example*, which Mama Mary urged us to pray, if want world peace. At one time, it captured the world's attention, when Fr. Paton led this crusade.

Nevertheless, it faded through the years and perhaps we can give it a second chance, especially now that the devil is in human forms, blowing up Christian churches. Many Christians in Syria were beheaded. Does this not awaken us to use our weapon, the Rosary, to *"Deliver us from evil?" (Anima Christi)*

During this time in history, when most men and women have necklaces without Jesus crucifix around their neck, it is because the Devil who appear in human being like us would make us feel embarrassed for doing so, instead "the Devils among us." I wonder why we should reflect their "embarrassment," when it in fact, this could be an opportunity for us to preach Jesus' Crucifixion on the Cross, as an example.

I ordered from Michael Warsaw, the Warrior Rosary that I would like to wear around my neck for life. I am sure I cannot do this without the grace of God, so help me Lord, that I may know <u>how to pray!</u> Amen.

❋

"SUFFER THE LITTLE CHILDREN"

Anyway, let us be satisfied for one drop of water in our understanding, what *faith* we have invested in the ocean of God's love and mystery. Or have we?

Remember, when the Apostles tried to drive the children around Jesus, what did Jesus say? He said, *"Suffer the little children to come to you for theirs is the kingdom of Heaven."*

After I read this I got a "lump" in my throat. Our present generation of children (2017) generally does not seem to reflect the "childlike innocence" of children where Christ thought that the "kingdom of Heaven" is theirs.

Last night, (9/29/14) Bill O'Reiley asked journalist Laura Ingram, a Catholic newscaster about children apparently hooked on cell phones. She said, when I arrived home definitely "cell phones are out" of the hand of my children.

When a family is together especially after work and after school, it's not only homework time for kids but a space where family interact their character and values to children who are growing up.

It reminded me what Queen Elizabeth who was famous for rearing great Prince and Princes was asked how she accomplished such great achievement and she answered in one short sentence, *"Give me the first seven years of a child and you can have the rest."*

My parents did this and though I am now exposed to the manifestation of evils in human forms, I find strength what my parents left me before they went to the other side. I look at this devils in human forms such as ISIS. If you know what I mean.

I remembered years back in our family gathering that whatever good and bad experiences we had during the day we ended up before the family's altar reciting the holy rosary together, 13 of us before going to bed. All of them, 13 brothers are now in the other side. None of them died in violence.

Recently, when I visited my good nephew his two older children kissed my hand as a sign of respect. But their 12-year-old kid did not even notice I entered the house: he was busy on cell phones entertaining himself on violent cartons.

I suppose that maybe majority when they grow up would give what they saw in violent cartons: they would be prone to quick temper and violence as many of us witness today. <u>They give what they often receive in mind thru cell phones.</u> The other problem here is that they have access for kids' entertainment laced with sexual suggestion.

So, what do you expect when they grow up: they have tendency to do violence, child porno they have access on that too. We therefore must expect violence as normal and certainly the lack of moral values.

During the time, Jesus told the Apostles about children "theirs is the kingdom of Heaven." Jesus wanted them to have the innocence of a child, to be childlike, not childish when approaching people for evangelization.

Therefore, with the kind of culture we have today, it is understandable that it would be difficult to evangelize a generation of me, myself and I personality - the product of cell phones. Ms. Laura Ingram is right; the little space of family interaction is important for children to know their parents' moral values.

NOTE: Parents who do not have moral values usually cannot give what they do not have.

✳

LAUGH & GROAN

Have you been a victim of circumstances? I was. Brod. Ondo (may he rest in peace) used to tell me, "*Elmer, laugh and the world will laugh at you; cry and you will cry alone.*" He said this because most often I was laughing at home. NOTE: If I did not laugh, often the slit in my left eye could be noticed; whereas, if I laughed, both eyes looked even like a Jap.

Maybe, while Brod. Ondo was on earth; he must have had a lot of experiences specially when he gave up his position as one of the administrators in Mati at the *First Insular Bank* and went to New York on a visitor's visa. In New York, he worked underground for several years without his family.

Not so much with me. But I could pull out two out of several incidents where I could *laugh or cry or groan* whenever I remember them. Before I cite specific over which you might perhaps laugh at my own expense (which I do not mind), allow me to condition your mind first.

It was one Christmas time when exploding firecrackers became a phenomenon at the Ateneo de Davao high school department. At first, our prefect of discipline, Fr. Webster (perhaps out of respect for the festive season) tolerated it.

But when it became disruptive to classes going on, Fr. Webster issued a decree which most of us viewed as a form of dictatorship and as unchristian. His decree was to ban firecrackers during the Christmas season. The decree was powerful: the loud explosions stopped for a couple of days.

With Christmas' lights were dancing on the mind of naughty boys like me, we found classes boring. I surely agreed with them. They re-grouped and planned. Although I was one of the naughtiest at home (almost every week I did receive a wacky on my back), I was not one of them.

The reason why I behaved in school was my eldest brother, Emelio, who was the school Registrar, was paying for my tuition and Brod. Lading's. I loved going to the school of the rich. And Brod. Emelio warned us that for any "foolishness" that would embarrass him, he would transfer us to the public school, generally the school of the "have nots."

I loved the Ateneo de Davao because while I almost belonged to the "have nots," at least I was studying in a school for wealthy families. I remember that during recess time, I stayed in my room while the rich boys would rush to the canteen and enjoy their snacks of cokes and sandwiches. These were little joys I could only wish for, but being poor I could only taste them in my imagination. Though my tummy was empty, at least my mind was full – if you know what I mean.

I am hesitating to tell you these two incidents but I

might as well, knowing we are one close-knit family. This is the first incident: Brod. Lading and I usually would bring our lunch of rice and one hard-boiled egg to school. During noon break we ate our lunch under the basketball bleachers.

But on one unfortunate occasion, while we went to the washroom, a dog picked up our lunch box. I had to chase the little scoundrel otherwise, I would go hungry for nothing. Of course, when the dog noticed that I ran faster than he, he dropped the box and sped away. I said to myself, "*Good thinking doggie or you get busted.*"

Well, we did not miss our lunch of egg and rice. However, there were rare occasions in which if our housemaid did not like our behaviors, she would pack for each of us a lunch box containing only corn and *bulad*. I could not complain, I was already under the bleachers, angry but hungry. I thought that maybe next time, if the dog would pick up our lunch box of corn and *bulad* he could have it. I might have to go on hunger strike.

Hence, I could therefore say that my studying in this school was more of a privilege, a favor granted. Anyway, since I could not afford being naughty in school, I made up for it at home. Which sometimes explained why we got a lunch box of corn (mauling lang sa tahop) and *bulad, ulo pa gayud*.

Our housemaid named Goring, came from Bohol. You know, during the time of Pres. Garcia, Bohol was known as a country "outside" of the Philippines. Anyway, every morning when Goring made her water, she would face east, where Bohol is located. I asked her why.

Goring seriously said that her father had given her the instruction that whenever she made water, she should face where she came from so that she would not get lost on her way home. It was a nice joke for me but not for her. She was a simple woman but not so smart when it came to our lunch box of corn and *bulad*.

The second incident happened when I was walking through the corridor of the school, a fire cracker exploded. It so happened that I was nearest to the explosion, but since I did not have any sense of guilt, I did not run away from the scene.

Other students, they were a bit far from the scene, scampered away, leaving me on the spot. Maybe, they thought I was a macho boy. Although I liked the idea - heh, heh.

When Fr. Webster saw me by myself and glanced at all the other boys, laughing and giggling in the distance, he (with clinched fist and tightened mouth) gestured me to come forward. And while I was explaining my innocence to which he had no ears, he collard me and brought me outside to the school-campus like a black sheep (I would rather say a black lamb) separated from the white flock.

At least, he gave little credence to my innocent look and explanation because he said that I would have just to stand in front of the school beside the flagpole so that if there was another firecracker explosion, I would be exonerated. Fair enough. Jesuits were known to be fair-minded.

I thought that was the end of the story. I did not know it was just a beginning, as after 15 minutes of my being at the flagpole and all classes resumed, there erupted multiple explosions of firecrackers beneath the car near me.

It was loud enough to disrupt the classes. I saw students looking out from the windows, pointing and laughing at me. Those who thought I was a "Macho" boy must have had their confirmation. Though I felt terrible, I loved the idea rather than to be called "<u>Machochita</u>," as I would fondly call Nong Boy "*kay pagka may tuya man ni.*"

As usual, I stood my ground because I was not the engineer of these mini-explosions. I was the wrong guy caught in the right place. Or I was the right guy caught in a wrong place. What I am trying to say – is that the situation that I was in, did not make any sense to me.

Then out of the door, Fr. Webster came, scratching his head with his eyes up to heaven he gestured for me to come in. I knew from his look that he did not have the slightest doubt that I did it. I told him, "*Father, it was a time bomb, believe me.*"

He looked at me hard and I noticed his eyes becoming blood shot with anger and frustration and seemed to say to me, "*You are telling me?*" So, from his body language he did not have an ear for me. He told me to join the other naughty boys punished for different "crimes" by walking endlessly around the school gym.

At the end of classes, I was selected for the whacking. We were brought inside an empty room. I was asked to bring down my pants and to position myself like a dog. Unfortunately, during my sophomore year I seldom wore a brief. I reserved it for Sunday Mass.

So, my bum was exposed naked for a better view. I wonder to this day if Father had a good laugh while I was preparing to groan upon the impact of the one meter wooden ruler.

I received 9 wacky: nearly hit the basket of my private part. Modesto, a naughty friend of mine, was next to me. He cried even just at the first wacky of his bum. He got only 5. I did not have such technique so that was perhaps why I got 9. Why?

Because at home if I would cry before the whacky hit my bum, Papa would repeat the count. I could not afford to cry or complain because I did not want a repeat. Why? Papa's "stick" was not a wooden one-meter ruler. It was a two-feet long hard private part of a cow. This one time short and soft private part of a cow was made long and hard when it was tied with a stone and hung from a coconut tree for 3 days under the heat of the sun.

Whenever it hit me, I would cry and say, "*Husto na patay nako.*" I resolved not to repeat the same "crime" like stealing money from our grocery store in Argao, but I would pilfer other items like chocolate or crackers.

One day I puffed on a "Diamond," a brand of cigar equal to Matam-is. I used to see people smoking and planned to try it myself. I stole one pack and consumed it under the coconut tree where the private part of the cow was hung, not far from home. After I consumed the whole pack, 20 sticks, my vision got blurry and I felt like vomiting and passing out. My conscience kept saying, "*Naga ba-an kay na ngawat man.*"

It was good I reached home, slept unnoticed and woke never to touch such stuff again until now at age 75. Anyway, I thought what others like Brod. Lading would have for a lifetime I got for 20 minutes under the coconut tree. Maybe, that is the reason why the pleasure of smoking has made Brod. Lading lived longer, and this prompts him sometimes to say, "To live longer is unnecessary," Heh, heh. Brod. lading is now 76 and counting years, and sticks of cigarettes.

I still fondly remember that as we were growing up, I thought that since I got taller than him I honestly thought that I would also overtake his age. I did realize later that the year would not stop to get me older than him.

To this day, whenever I remember Fr. Webster's ruler and my smoking episode, I would simply <u>laugh</u>. But if I remember my Papa's "stick," I would *groan* over the loss of my childhood vices, which loss instead of being traumatized, gracefully helped to shape me into real "Macho" inside for "<u>Ad Majoren Dei Gloriam.</u>"

❋

DEATH WISH

1. Ven. Bishop Fulton J. Sheen

It was probably March, when I remembered the late Ven. Bishop Fulton J. Sheen's talked in the 1950's NBC television network. He spoke to 20 million viewers about his death wish.

He said it clearly with his beautiful baritone voice that he wished to die in one of the feast days of our Lady, otherwise he would complain in Heaven.

He got his wish when he was found dead on December 9th, the feast day of our Lady of America, in the private chapel of his New York residence.

Although unholy compared with Bishop Sheen and like the thief on the right side of Christ in Calvary, I said, "Lord, I would like to die on the 19th of March, the feast day of my St. Joseph, a martyr defending the honor of our Lady."

I was born in 1937 and for my death wish, I left the year to God, the Father, who created me. So, unlike Bishop Sheen if I won't make it on March 19th (unworthy as I am for this gift), I won't complain in case I would be in Heaven.

As a human being like us, Jesus said in his agony at the

Garden of Gethsemane, "My Father, if it is possible let this cup pass from me; nevertheless, not as my will but as thou will." (Matthew 26: 39-40)

Knowing the pain and suffering on this road to Calvary, Jesus pleaded with bloody tears on his face for the 2nd time but God, the Father, refused him, his only precious gift for our own salvation.

Hence, every March 19th that passes by I look forward for another year to enjoy life, rather than the Jesuit's dictum, which I learned in one of the retreats at the Ateneo de Davao, Philippines, "To live life as if it is your last day."

Why did I choose the feast day of St. Joseph? Simple. St. Joseph never failed to answer me, especially during some of the life-threatening events that I have encountered in my life.

For example, I prayed daily for more than 10 years that we would win the case of our only daughter, who died at the age of 38 due to the negligence of two doctors.

If we are not doctors, we would not have discovered it. Our lawyer after knowing the case said that it was a hard one to win. He suggested to arrange a settlement instead. With all disrespect to our good lawyer, we refused and pursued the case.

At the end of more than ten years of praying to St. Joseph, the judge and the jury ruled in our favor. So now, you understand why in gratitude to St. Joseph, I would like to die on his feast day, March 19th.

2. Mother Angelica of the EWTN

Now, in comparison about death of Mo. Angelica of the EWTN, who passed away at age of 92, March 27th 2016, Easter Sunday, she did not choose a day when to die. What was common between them: both practiced what they preached and lived a life sublime.

For fair and balance, I am mentioning this point of distinction because many of us (me excluded) have not decided the day of our departure from this world into our life eternal.

Many of us, like Mo. Angelica just leave to God the decision as to when we will die. I've chosen when to die. I chose March 19th so I could prepare my soul, not only on my "last day" but the whole year through after the 19th of March.

Unlike Ven. Bishop F. Sheen, Mo. Angelica was like most of us, she did not choose the day of her departure just as God has decided for her the day of her existence. She trusted with great faith, her last day on earth.

Since Mo. Angelica after a busy day of broad casting, rubbing elbows with workers and media people, hearing bad remarks about her, she must had been angry inside to say that she would not make it to Heaven, but be "lucky" if she would end up in Purgatory. After all, she argued, after Purgatory was Heaven.

When Pope Francis heard of her passing, he unequivocally said, "Mo. Angelica is in Heaven." Hence, if in fact Mo. Angelica is in Purgatory she can complain to our Lord, saying that Pope Francis' 'infallibility' seems to have guaranteed her a place in Heaven.

And what seemed to be an amazing grace, most media agreed with Pope Francis. After all, as a matter of conscience what suffering some of them did to her, there was still room of good will.

Not to mention the many miracles in her life time, did not Baby Jesus turn live before Mo. Angelica when she visited Italy and told her to build a Temple? And Mo. Angelica did so in Alabama. Then how can Baby Jesus not welcome her in Heaven?

3. My "Death Wish" In Jeopardy?

I. Introduction:

Before I end this article allow me to tell you an almost tragic true story of my life. One bright Sunday morning I felt it was most ideal to go to Massena, a 45-minute drive from Ogdensburg, New York.

After being preoccupied and obsessed for days on end, I wanted to go to Massena to try recover my wallet which I left it at the counter in the Fam Dollar Store.

However, my wife wanted to go to Watertown. instead. Any other day Watertown would be fine, not on this particular day. Nevertheless, "stuff" like this was something I could not tell my wife.

Otherwise, one bright morning might turn dark and rainy. Experience is my biggest teacher for 41 years of beautiful marriage, heh, heh.

You know, recently (off the record) I just made a promise to our Lord that I was giving up as one of the children of the Father of lies, Satan, my long lost but insisting "friend."

II. <u>A White Lie That Did Not Work</u>:

I thought in this circumstance, one 'white lie' might hide the truth as it did successfully on several occasions. So, in a diplomatic way, I said,

"Mel, there is a pant at TG Max (her favorite store) that I want to buy."

After what seemed a friendly argument, back and forth, I gave up before I might spoil the day. So, I would tell her the truth that I left my wallet at the Fam Dollar store beside TG Max.

I expected for her to raise her voice pluperfect but perhaps for my benefit that I already lost my wallet I was spared of what might have been a good teaching lesson, heh, heh.

Then, she said, *"Instead of going there, why don't you call the store to save us a trip?"* A simple good idea my brain missed. Not unusual.

"No, I can't," I said. *"You know I can talk but even with my hearing aid I cannot hear. My hearing aid whistles the moment it gets contact
with the telephone."*

Well, she looked for the telephone number and inquired. The store at the counter said, *"Sorry, we found no black wallet."*

That seemed to settle the argument and I just tried to relax in spite of the fact that it contained her ID card with address over the idea *"Finder's keeper."*

II: <u>On the Narrow Road to Watertown</u>:

So, Imelda turned the car driving unaware that this way to Watertown might have been our last journey on earth, including perhaps our three lovely dogs, named – Happy, the daughter of Sandy, a pure Shih Tzu, and her husband, a 12 lbs. white curly Lhasa.

Anyway, after driving the speed limit of 55-60
Mph we arrived in Watertown from Ogdensburg in 54 Minutes; nothing tragic which we were not aware had happened.

Not far from the Gasoline Station the traffic was bumper to bumper. So, Imelda applied her brake and was surprised the brake pedal went as deep as she could and lighted, *"NO BRAKE FLUID."*

So, she just turned right at the gasoline station for a

service. We thought that a simple adding of brake fluid would suffice. The service man brought a bottle of brake fluid, opened the hood
and presto, poured it. And he was stunned: the whole bottle was swallowed up faster than he anticipated.

He went back and got another bottle. He poured it and the same thing happened. Suspicious, he checked down below and saw all the fluid on the cement floor.

I heard him say that we must be travelling for hours without brake fluid. And he could not believe how we made it. He suggested to go at the repair shop across the street for a checkup.
Sure enough there was a big tear that the whole system had to be replaced. After almost 3 hours, the job was done. During these hours, I asked Imelda if she did not apply the brake during that 54-minute drive.

She did, but the "No Brake Fluid" sign was noted. It was only near the gas station that when she applied the brake and the warning showed up.

III: <u>The Miracle, If You Consider</u>:

No doubt about it, though I felt unworthy, I was certain we were travelling under the guidance of Heaven. If you have any other explanation write to me.

For me, had we met an accident on this particular day my wife and I would have been dead, not to mention part of our life – the three lovely "kids" on board.

Both of us could not comprehend how we had been travelling safely for 54 minutes with the speed of 55-60 mph and no hint of impending tragedy.

I would not say, "*We were lucky.*" I could not say by conscience without undermining God's divine providence which generally often spared those who loved him.

It slowly came 'simmering' with pain and thanks giving into my senses why on earth we were spared from a fatal accident on this particular Sunday.

Was it because, modesty aside, I usually would spend 3-4 hrs. praying every morning starting most often at 2:30 AM reciting the Rosary. My 'Superego' (if I had) said clearly, "NO." You see, I was so wrapped up with material thing, like my lost wallet that I neglected my spiritual life.

It is like when you are very rich and there is nothing to ask God because you can afford, hence there is no place in your heart to pray to God. In that way, you neglected your soul.

Your soul would be NO different than like those famous singers of "pop and fun" and actors and millionaires whose soul are empty and look for Heaven through opioid and marijuana that if they do not ask for mercy at the last moment, there is no doubt they are on their way to Hell. A little experience compared the suffering of their soul prior death.

IV: The "Shock" in Our Journey:

Anyway, to continue our journey I did not know the date of this day. At age 78, still going strong with pace maker it seemed I was qualified not to be blamed. I said,

"Mel, do you know what date is today?" She replied, "It's March 19, why?" I was so wrapped up with material thing, like my lost wallet that I could not understand how come I did not remember it was March 19, 2016, feast of my <u>St. Joseph</u>. He reminded me of his love that I perhaps assumingly but unintentionally forgot.

St. Joseph must have thought beside the fact that perhaps I was not spiritually ready for Purgatory he could not afford my wife to die and see me where I would have been. Praise the Lord through my St. Joseph, my family's patron Saint, once more out of many near death experiences I was saved. Alleluia!

V: The Concept of "Holiness:" or Better of "Sainthood."

<u>Note</u>: Don't ever think that since I see souls from the other side, objectively I am a holy person or that I am nearer to God than you. I think <u>the opposite is true</u>. How come?

Take for example what Jesus said, *"Blessed are those who see and believe but <u>more blessed</u> are those who do not see and believe."*

I think it's only *common sense* that people like me who see souls from the other side (though not too often) needs this grace because I see and believe. I am therefore <u>weaker</u> before the eyes of God than those who do not see and believe.

Just as those who see and take advantage to change their soul becomes a Saint much more so for those who are more blessed who do not see and believe. If they would take advantage to further walk on the narrow road to holiness they could become the greatest Saint in our time like the only son of a very wealthy man decades ago, Francis of Assisi.

My conclusion is: develop with the grace of God that when you love Him with your whole heart and mind even the concept of sacrifice associated with love is unworthy of the idea that your love of God has become unconditional.

Be generous to me if some of my ideas need purifications. My e-mail is *e_abear@hotmail.com*. May I hear from you? Thanks.

✳

THE ROCK OF THE CHURCH

When people heard what he just said, "*I am the bread of life who came down from Heaven (John 6:35)* (as perhaps we would exactly do if we were in that crowd) they said, "*This man is crazy*." They lingered for a while, what more this Son of a carpenter from poor Nazareth would say. And Jesus said:

"*He who believes in me will have life everlasting and I will raise him up in the last days (John 6:35)*."

That made it worse. They understood (as some of us today might not) that once dead how could he be risen? Jesus was certainly perceived as a dreamer. People walked away. At least one hundred disciples left. Jesus did not attempt to say, "*Wait, let me explain*."

Only the 12 Apostles remained with him. And Jesus asked them: "*Will you also go away? (John 6:66-67)*." But Simon Barjona replied, "*To whom shall we go, you have the word of eternal life*." And Jesus told Simon, "*Flesh and blood had not revealed it to you but my heavenly Father (Matthew 16:18)*."

After Jesus said this, he changed the name of Simon to Peter and appointed him as the first Pope. Ven. Bishop Sheen commented that among the unbroken chain of Popes, St. Peter was the weakest, had it not that Jesus was holding his hand.

❋

THE BREAD OF LIFE

After God created a beautiful world on the 5th day *(Genesis 1:23)*, He said the next day: *"Let us create a man in our own <u>image and likeness</u>… male and female, He created them (Genesis 1:26-27)."*

On the 7th day, God rested *(Genesis 2:2)*. He told them to enjoy in the Garden of Paradise except not to touch one apple tree (which still stands today in Iraq). Sad to say, our first parents, named Adam and Eve failed. They ate to their heart's content. *Wala koyape!*

Therefore, God's *<u>image and likeness</u>* were graces taken away from them and indefinitely down to our present generation. Unless, we are born again by the baptism of either <u>*water, fire or desire*</u> we remain out of grace and out of Heaven. If you do not believe this reality in the afterlife, "you will believe it." As Padre Pio said, *"When you will be there (in hell)."*

However, God's infinite love for us, which is beyond Satan's comprehension brought his only son, Jesus Christ, to redeem us by dying on the cross, so we won't end up in Hell, which Satan had created and prepared for his followers. God did not create Hell but allowed Satan to do so. Unfortunately, we do create Hell ourselves, when we no longer believe in Heaven afterlife. Satan can take his vacation.

Anyway, how did Jesus become **"The Bread of Life?"**

Let us recall the time when Moses came to liberate the Jews from the Egyptian's rule. While traveling on their way to Israel, they run out of food. One of them asked Moses:

"*Moses, we are hungry.*" And Moses asked God, and <u>bread came down like rain from Heaven</u> *(Exodus 6:31)* and people forgot their hunger as they panicked and filled their backpacks and their tummies up to the brim. Now, decades later in Jesus' life he was asked with the same challenge.

A man who might have known Moses' story asked Jesus probably with sarcasm: "*Jesus, we are hungry. Send us some bread from Heaven!*"

Jesus looked at him straight in the eye and the crowd around him. He wanted to be sure that they would hear it <u>loud and clear</u> when he solemnly declared: "*I am the **Bread of life** who came down from Heaven (John 6:35).*"

Today, we are privileged to be God's recipient of His grace. Every Mass a priest in persona Christi changes bread to Christ's own body, and wine into his own blood. Because this is the mystery of faith, it is an open field for the fools to interpret according to his own status quo.

❅

"IS LIFE WORTH FIGHTING FOR?"

Is it? This title reminds me of an incident during my teaching years in Padada, Davao. To recall, during my academic years (per introduction) I was an average student in High School. I know that is not a news, heh, heh.

Though I managed (less study) my rational Philosophy and Religion were almost flat one. I was poor particularly in Physics where I failed because as simple as the metaphor of 5+5, I could not understand why a Chinese man after searching his pockets got it right, as = 11?

Anyway, after my B.S. and senior B.S.E with honors, I got a teaching job in Padada, Davao. Modesty aside, since most students were generally average, I found myself it seemed as one of the best teachers in town.

I literally memorized my lesson plan of the day. With good expression, who does not love good impression from students? As my Papa used to tell me whenever I made excuses, "*Elmer, in the land of the blind, ang bulhog ma-oy Hari.*"

This incident happened: The third-year high school boys at St. Michael High School were so unruly that one teacher after another left, some crying. They could not stand this class. As a last resort, Sister Jean called me to handle this class. I was teaching Religion and English, not my science major.

It was true, these boys were mostly "crack pots" that every time I wrote on the black board, chalks would rain in. As I would turn around, Good Grief, - they looked like saints "ironically" from the Hades. Nobody was brave enough to squeal in my favor. I could not blame anyone of them. Why?

I remembered as an amateur "crack pot" myself that I used to, back in my high school days, I used to rejoice with Roberto who would shout at Fr. Webster, whenever he turned his back on us, "Opao!" Why? He had few hairs dangling mercilessly around his head, his top, the calvarium looked like a shining landing pad for red flies to wash their dirty hands.

Anyway, I finally caught one in action throwing a chalk. I told him harshly, "*Get out*" and he did. The whole class was stunned. No teachers had done that. Not to this boy. The next day he came back with a pistol in his belt: he obviously inserted it that in such a way I would not miss.

In my childhood, I recalled that I never ran away from a fight (though seldom) whenever I was right. I learnt that from my Father who spent his time every 4:00 AM reading "*The Imitation of Christ*" by Thomas à Kempis. And he added that I should be humble to admit whenever I was wrong.

With all the nerves, high among his classmates I came near him and said: "*If you won't fire that pistol to me right now it is plastic.*" I knew it was not plastic from my

ROTC experience.

But I thought that I had to give up my life for a simple "nut" like this one for what I thought was the right thing to do. He stood up, all anxious and nervous eyes were focus on us as to who would blink first. I was ready for a fight if needed. It did not happen. He blinked.

Instead of pulling the pistol to fire at me he turned back and went home. From that day on, I was teaching to this group who behaved like saints ironically from Heaven. NOTE: That student who threatened me with a pistol was the son of the town's Mayor in Padada, Davao.

All the while Sister Jean was behind the window at the back of the class (I did not notice) told me later and said (perhaps she did not notice the tense moment),

"How did you handle these rough boys. They are so attentive in your class." I just smiled. I could have said, *"God be praised he spared my life, for something ahead I'd no idea."*

I wished this true incident had ended. Several years after I returned to Padada to visit Nonoy-Lily de Los Reyes' wonderful Family, where I boarded during a year of my teaching, I saw from a gas station a man. He was running toward me as I alighted from the bus. I recognized him as the boy with a pistol in his belt. I thought that he was out for a revenge but to my surprise he gave me a warm hug and said, *"Welcome, Sir!"*

That Sunday I attended Mass. I did not see him but I saw several of my students who were my fans. After

Mass, they did not even bother to smile or greet me. I felt so bad, it would have been better if I did not know them at all.

Sorry for your time, reading one of the many unwritten incidents in my life. Now, I know that I am nearing our Lord in the other side, wisdom made me realize that *__Life, indeed, (according to Bishop F. Sheen) is worth living.__* And if I may add, *__Worth fighting for.__*

❋

MOTHER MARY
"REFUGE OF SINNERS"
Pray for Us

In our journey through life, we often do things with good intentions. Sometimes, it would end up with great success. You want names from Las Vegas? Or names of Kings under a star of Bethlehem?

At other times, success would turn into a tragedy. You want names from Hollywood? Between these odds, the good people will pursue on their narrow path with hope and prayer for the best yet to come from God through Mary's rosary.

For example: My wife and I bought a 960 sq.m. lot on a top of a small hill, facing the sea not far off, in Argao. It was meant someday for me to rest and to retire. We brought in relatives and friends to climb and view this place.

Magnificent, they said (notwithstanding that I tripped on a dead twig on my way up. Yes, I stumbled and to the dead twig's success my demise made me fall flat on my back in front of everybody). *Magnificent, was it? This place,*" I said to myself, "*needs to be exorcised.*"

Shaking and brushing off my mess, I stood up and pretended there was no bruise nor pain. Just dry leaves clinging to my shirt and pant. *Macho*! I thought. An expression I was used to what impression I might get from people around me. But now, I was nothing but a *Machochita*

I glanced furtively at the dead twig and murmured, *"Stronger than myself, eh! It did not break, image of ghost."* By then, I joined the laughter. My pretension worked. *(You know, I should have cried, with blood beneath my shin bone of my pant).*

Time passed swiftly. Yesterday was forgotten. Tomorrow was coming. Today, I remembered one of my visits to Nabunturan, Davao to see my favorite only sister, Carmencita and Brother in Law Catalino. She was a college professor with Ph.D. degree in social communication, graduated AB, B.S.E. cum laude. She wanted to retire after decades of teaching.

Seeing her aging situation, I was convinced later in my heart that Argao would be the best place for them to rest and retire with me. Nabunturan was isolated and many people were thriving in poverty except those who cut the logs for export abroad.

I told them to leave Nabunturan, invested 3200K in fact, for them to settle and be happy on top of a hill overlooking the rice field *(living to my principle that true happiness comes from making others happy).*

Hence, reciprocity was not on my mind who had been trying to empty myself with St. Francis of Assisi as my model of perfection (which later through no fault of St. Francis I changed to St. Therese, the little flower).

I believed what my prayerful sister said that it was an answer to her prayer for years, a dream came true. Can you believe? She wrote to me later that I was an Angel sent to her by God? Oh, my Lord!

"*Do angels have money?*" I asked myself. I always asked myself whenever I could not answer simple question like that. Hence, when Mo. Angelica's network would be closed at 5 PM if she could not produce 300K.

Before 5 PM a box arrived (which did not have a label where it came from). She counted over many dusty dollars and it was exactly 300K. No doubt on her mind the Angels must have picked it up across America. Therefore, Angels don't have money.

Nevertheless, her prayer and dream, and my 300K went up literally in flame as if its black smoke came from Hell. Why? Because after a year they left the place in a hurry, back to Nabunturan where the poor thrived spiritually better than those who might have little money perhaps like me. I did not understand, I asked myself, "*Did some dead twig come to life?*" No malice intended.

Yet, should we say, *kind of whose reflection, eh*? God seemed to speak: after all, the place was not meant for them. Then, for whom? I did not want to think what Ernest Hemingway would say, "*For whom the bell tolls...,* it tolls for thee, man." The will of God has many dark corners along its way to Heaven; but it's not for us to question but accept and offer the future to God in trust.

Recently, I came back to Argao with Mark, my nephew. We climbed the hill and carefully watch dead twigs along the way. When we arrived at the top we discovered a small lamp, casting light in one shadowed corners of the unfinished concrete structure.

The lamp was an expression of hope and perhaps with a broken dream but unbroken love. *Something must have happened on this spot*, I thought. The place felt eerie as few white dyed hairs on my balding head stood up half way. I did not know the reason why.

A skinny man approached us and said that a wealthy married woman (by Argao's standard) nearby took a poison perhaps out of family misunderstanding and came on this hill perhaps in search peace where it appeared there was none at home. On this spot where a lamp was lighted she passed away.

I visited her family to express my deep condolence. A little girl about 6 years old perhaps not knowing that she had no more Mommy to call came to me and turned back to her father who I thought appeared remorseful. He had a boat for big fishing beside the house. I thought the family was well up.

Anyway, bothered after more than a week at home I came back with Mark, my nephew, with holy water to bless the place and Mo. Mary's rosary on hand. Upon arrival, there was a still the small lamp flickering among the shadowed lane of the structure. The lamp was an incense of continued prayer, lifting up to Heaven from what might seem, a hellish part of the earth.

I sprinkled the place with holy water and together we recited the sorrowful mystery, hoping that the woman who found refuge on this hill to pray that she might find her restless heart at peace. A place where hope there seemed none, where one's fate appeared forever sealed hopefully in union with God's will, and God forbid, not in union with Satan's will.

Keeping in mind, that all the drops of the entire ocean when taken together could not contain the mercy and love of God. That was what the *contradiction* on Calvary was all about, ringing through centuries that the Truth in Mary's heart might be revealed. Was it ever, in the fullness of time?

As soon as we started praying the rosary of Mama Mary the fresh air from the sea I breathed faded away as if some dark power brought in the odor of a burning rotten flesh, urging me to stop praying the rosary or risk breathing. I took the risk out of grace to break the spell.

"The woman is hopeless, queried unsolicited word from someone's mind in me. And I dare say, why the odor fighting against Mama Mary's rosary, weapon of Satan's destruction breaking the abode of his being, the unsanctified odor of this lost angel of death?" I argued.

I defied the moment of dark sinister air and persevered: at this very moment, I prayed louder to crowd over the insurgent cries of what seemed a feeling of anger, bitterness and despair, a disturbance that for sure was not of my own making.

Towards the end of the rosary the odor of a burning rotten flesh (that Mark later experienced too) faded away. And once again, I experienced the breath of fresh wind passing through Camellia trees from the sea nearby.

Suddenly, I was reminded that I took refuge on this hill to pray for a sinner just like me. I have a plan to build a Monastery on this hell, I mean, on this hill, quoting one of Mama Mary's titles, *"Refuge of sinners." Alleluia!*

On March 15, 2009, a Monastery named after St. Michael stood awesome overlooking the sea, the rice field, the mango trees and people nearby especially near the house of Mayor Edsel Galeos, my great grandnephew who called me, Uncle Elmer.

On this date, too, a celebration of this Monastery took place attended by notable people from the community and from Cebu city and people from abroad. This was the occasion when St. Michael Monastery was dedicated to our late daughter Rossana Abear Surujedeo.

The St. Michael's Monastery was in this occasion donated to the Society of Angel of Peace founded by my Apo whom later I knew was related to me from the Espina's generation. Praise the Lord!

❄

ON HELL & PURGATORY

When the 3 little children of Fatima, Jacinta, Lucia, and Francisco saw Hell, where souls were forever suffering and lost, they collapsed. So, Mama Mary had to stop the vision.

That is so because the pain and suffering of Purgatory according to St. Faustina is the same as Hell. The only difference is that people in Purgatory are suffering with joy that one day they would join with Jesus and the Saints in Heaven.

NOTE: Their stay in Purgatory is shortened if you pray for them. I never miss a day not praying the souls in Purgatory especially for those I do not know.

By the way, what is purgatory like? It is a place where our souls are further purified for a hundred years or a thousand, depending how much sins they have had in their heart to be clean out. It is like the dirtier a pant is the longer the washing takes place. I don't mean your pant. I mean my pant since I used to change only once a week before.

We, therefore clean our souls because Jesus said "*No one can enter the gate of Heaven who is not (clean) perfect.*" In other words, who is not a Saint.

And if I keep being smart like Satan by telling even

a white lie it would come with pain in purgatory but associated with hope and joy to be in Heaven. And you know what? I will do - penance to remove prevent callous in my soul. In other words, I pray:

Soul of Christ sanctify me
to purify my bones, nerves, brain
So, I will have a new strength
And enthusiasm of a new life.

Water from the side of Christ wash me
Be the water that quenches
My physical and spiritual thirst of thee
So, I will stand clean and radiant
Before your heavenly Father in Heaven.

Passion of Christ
Be the inspiration and power
That I might be able to overcome
The stress and strain of my life.

"Oh good Jesus, hear me
Suffer me not to be separated from thee
From the wicked enemy defend me
At the hour of my death
Call me and allow me to come to thee
That with your Saints I may praise thee,
Forever and ever. Amen." (Anima Christi).

❋

OF PATIENCE & ANGER

However, my persistence to commit sin is for others to develop <u>patience</u> with me, a virtue that makes a person holy and pleasing to God (as Jesus, himself, was patient when he was scourged for 33 lashes on his back).

Jesus could turn this soldier to stone like he and his Father did when the wife of "Jacob" turned around and saw the fire falling on the city of Sodom and Gomorrah. But for our sake he remained patient. He expects us to do the same with others, friends or foe.

Patience makes us cool and calm in spite of burning anger from inside. If you control anger you express patience. While anger leads to violence, patience leads to understanding and love. This is the only way to go Heaven.

It does mean that we will allow people to give us lashes even if we are not at fault. We have to explain the truth. And the truth will soften the heart of those who want to do harm on us.

Let us have more <u>insight</u> about anger. When anger is let out it expresses violence toward others. And violence is a sin. Truly, anger, despair, hopelessness are properties within the heart of Satan, while patience, peace, and love are the properties of the angel in us that guide us in our journey to Heaven.

We are basically angels. If we do not allow Satan to get inside us. It is our choice not Satan. We give him the **key** to enter our heart and that key is anger. I am not saying that it is entirely wrong to be <u>angry</u>. There is such thing as healthy anger.

Let me explain it further: Remember, Jesus was angry when he saw people gambling inside his Father's house and he drove them away. Here, Jesus was angry but not for himself, but as Ven. Bishop Sheen said, he was angry ***not on behalf of himself but angry <u>on behalf of his Father</u>***.

In the same way, you can be angry on behalf of your Mom when she would suffer the unjust attack of others and not angry on behalf of yourself. For example, Dr. Jose Rizal and Sen. Benigno Aquino died on behalf of our country to save us from dictatorship and not on behalf of themselves. Were they able to save us?

Anyway, when Jesus was scourged 33 times he was not angry because he was <u>obedient</u> to his Father's will in Heaven. You know during the time of Jesus; 12 lashes were enough to kill a person.

The soldier was apparently told to stop the scourging of Jesus (2nd decade of the sorrowful mystery) because Jesus had still to carry the Cross up on the mountain to Calvary where he would be crucified to save us from our sins. Hell, I repeat, was not created by Jesus. It was created by Satan.

Sometimes, I wish I were Jesus because I do not have to carry a heavy Cross. Why? 12 lashes would be enough to kill me, right? And I won't be hanging on the cross on Calvary. Unlike me, Jesus is God and could stand 33 lashes for our own sake that we may not end up in Hell forever after our short journey on earth.

✻

For meditation only: recommendation, half a day after each number. I encourage you to challenge me with your questions. My e-mail: e_abear@hotmail.com

"PRAY WITHOUT CEASING"

(1) Aristotle wrote: *"Two contraries cannot co-exist in the same subject."* Exception: a person may look ugly outside but beautiful inside. They do co-exist in our being. But sooner or later, death will come.

And whether beauty will triumph at the end and or ugliness shall forever prevail is beyond us: the future can be predicted, assumed or even taken for granted but it is not our mortal eyes to see, *"Whatever will be will be."*

(2) What actually Aristotle meant is beyond the metaphysical, that is, **contraries inside our soul**. Our soul is a mixture of virtue and vice. As Fr. Ron Rolheiser wrote, *"...it is a mixture of grace and sin, of saint and sinner."*

When Jesus said, *"No one can enter the gate of Heaven who is not perfect,"* we scramble how to live a perfect life. The idea not to give up, in my part, has Blessed Pope John Paul II's, Splendor of Truth, my inspiration to try on what seems humanly *"impossible to achieve."*

I said, *"Impossible to achieve"* when I heard Jesus remarked, *"Without me you can do nothing."* Therefore, unlike Pope John Paul II who lived a perfect life, most of us, would someday die as imperfect souls.

(3) The prayer of Padre Pio would remind us God's three attributes: **mercy, forgiveness, and love.** There is no mention of the word, "**justice.**"
For if God will render justice to our performance who among us will be saved?

Hence, out of mercy, forgiveness, and love, Purgatory was created. To leave us no doubt of its existence the innocence of three little children in Fatima who knew nothing about rationalization was shown by our Lady.

Mind you, Purgatory is not God's justice: it is an expression of His ultimate and undying **divine mercy** for all of us. To leave us no doubt again this was revealed in 1937 by our Jesus, Himself, to St. Faustina.

(4). The question now is: How can we weed out de-sanctifying sin and stay in the state of sanctifying grace without using the art of rationalizations? Henri Newman wrote, "*We want to be great saints but we also don't want to miss out all the sensations that sinners experience.*" This wisdom of Henri Newman was conveyed to me recently by e-mail from my nephew, Rolly Bachiller who resides in Manila, Philippines.

I wanted to answer him but my wisdom as usual came late (if it is wisdom) a script from the aging gray matter of my brain. I would have e-mailed back and said, "*Wait until you will be nearing 80's a lot of foolish emotions would give way to dryness that no sensations could be awakened for experiences to occur, if you know what I mean.*"

There is only one outstanding solution out of many

that both Saints - Paul and Padre Pio subscribed: **"Pray without ceasing."** Make this prayer as G.M. Hopkins, SJ. wrote a *"habit of perfecting"* your soul. Hence, the danger of our failure to weed out sin is when **we stop praying.** Yet, prayer can be boring if one does not ask for the grace how to pray from the heart.

(5) So, one of the apostles realizing that without Jesus he could do nothing asked him, *"Lord, how do I pray?"* And Jesus answered, *"When you pray say, "**Our Father who art in Heaven hollowed be thy name thy Kingdom come thy will be done on earth as it is in Heaven.**"*

That is, contraries inside our souls cannot exist because when God dwells in our souls as we pray no demons could stand it. Our souls then become God's own Kingdom, either in Heaven or on earth, where His blessing is a light that guides us in our narrow path to Heaven.

Since singing is the highest form of prayer may I sing this song (if you stand my voice) for you:

When you stop to pray
Your soul will go astray
Wild horses of temptations
Are sensations beyond your control?
Unless you sing the "Our Father"
The kingdom of darkness shall prevail.

❈

PARKING LOT MIRACLE

As a background, I worked as a security patrol officer for one of the largest computer technology provider in the world. In any given time, my work place could have thousands of cars parked in huge and sprawling parking lots. We often, followed terminated employees and get their vehicle information for security reasons. Terminated employees who gave threats and caused trouble were monitored in the parking lot as they leave.

@ 4:00 pm, May 11, 2015, I was driving a patrol car when my supervisor called me. He showed me a picture of a male employee whose employment would be terminated at 5:00 pm later. My supervisor's order was, when he leaves the building I would follow him to his car and record the car's plate number.

My employer does this from time to time when thy feel the need for more information and trace the dismissed employee. Getting a car's plate number is a challenge especially when the car is moving.

You only have a few seconds to read and memorize the plate. To make matters more difficult, the bosses were monitoring the event and were waiting for the car information. I said to myself, "*I cannot fail.*"

Since there were 3 employee-access doors in the building office where the would be terminated employee worked at, each patrol officer was assigned a door to watch. When I got to my assigned door, the parking lot leading from the door was vast and there were about an estimated of 200 cars on the lot.

I said to myself, if our target person parked here, his car could be one of these 200 cars. Then I must be able to spot him early while walking so I could follow him to his car. I looked around for a vantage parking spot with an angle to see him coming.

My heart was racing as the 5:00 pm was nearing, and I was in a panic to really find a good spot. I was moving from one to spot to another. All this time, I was praying for the Holy Spirit and the angels to help me. A prayer usually said in times of crises.

Finally, I parked on a spot where I thought was the best. In so doing, I blocked a car parked in a stall. I thought I would just move if the car owner would come to move his car. Staying in that spot I continued to pray, "Please *Holy Spirit let me get that car info; please Holy Spirit and my angels don't let me fail.*"

Then a radio message came from another patrol officer positioned in front of the building. He said that the target subject had come out of the building and was heading to my parking lot. My heart raced at about 120 mph. I waited for a few seconds and soon enough our target came into view.

I was stunned to see that he was walking towards me and I thought if he would pass me, I would have to turn the car around and follow him. Then anything could happen, like me missing his car. He came walking right in front of me, his faced looked solemn and I knew why it was.

Then he came to the right side of my car and opened the car that I blocked. He could not get out of his parking stall unless I moved my car. I realized I was dead on blocking the person's car while praying to the Holy Spirit and angels to help me.

No doubt, the Holy spirit and my angels guided me to where I parked after my moving around to find the perfect spot. They delivered my target subject right in front of me and I got all the time to record his plate number.

So, I moved my car after noting his car plate. I purposely did not report over the radio my success in getting the info. A radio call came in asking if I was able to accomplish my mission. I said, "I did." I heard a comment in the background, "Good". I knew whose voice was that. It was my boss who was monitoring the surveillance.

And I did not care much. I was not in the business of wanting to be recognized and praised. I just did my job well with the blessing of the Holy Spirit and the angels. And they gave me a miracle.

Looking back at this amazing event, I asked how could I have parked and blocked that one specific car unknowingly that is was what I was looking for? One car to block out of about 200 cars? My prayer was one of being so dependent on the Holy Spirit and the angels. And no doubt they guided me. I felt so blessed.

❋

By: C. O. Abear

ON "HONEST IGNORANCE"

I. Here is my thought (maybe an ignorant thought) with regards to the topic of "Honest Ignorance" when Jesus, dying on the cross said to His Heavenly Father, "Father, forgive them for they do not know what they do." *(Matthew 4:5).*

I would presume that this soldier who pierced Jesus' heart on the cross must had heard about Jesus' sermon of the mount and miracles. Jesus was the new talk in Capernaum, the center of the city during those times when people from the North, South, West, and East met and exchanged the best of their respective arts and cultures.

For this particular soldier because he had not seen and witnessed seemed to him the fairy tale of rumors for example: as to how Jesus fed 5,000 people with one of his apostles distributing from one basket, bread and fried fish, and later beyond belief gathered 7 baskets full of left over.

Even today, I think, no one can handle that story except if one has the faith of Peter who walked on water to reach Jesus' helping hand. You know what happened when Peter doubted Jesus' gift of faith? He sunk. When in doubt like you and me.

And what more when Jesus, not minding that Lazarus

had been dead for days now must had smelled badly. Of course, their anticipation of what some of them regarded as an "exercise in futility" went sour when Lazarus came out of the grave with both hands raised up for the greater glory of Jesus. Yet it remained a rumor to this particular soldier whose duty was to pierce Jesus' heart.

So, I am pretty sure, this Torturer, a high ranking Roman soldier, must have had an idea stuck on his 'honest' head who was this man, dead on the Cross (as he had done many in the past) to see to it, not only to confirm that he was dead but that his heart was pierced as a routine procedure for the worst of criminals all for the glory of King Herod.

When he did this "blood and water" came pouring out between his rib, a flick of mini drop fell upon his eyes, which opened his sight that Jesus looked at him alive with deep compassion. After this fate, deeply regretful and weary, he went home with a broken heart repaired after what grace could do to a fate done out of honest ignorance.

Later, tradition might not have recorded that it was possible he was one of the many nameless Christian soldiers fighting against a well-armed Romans soldiers in the amphitheater to entertain King Herod's vanity of vanities.

II. When Satan Identified himself

I remember from EWTN, from Father Barron, that in an exorcism done on a demon possessed when asked who were the devils inside the person, one of the evil spirits proudly identified himself as one of the soldiers (who crowned Jesus with thorns).

NOTE: Did the devil tell the truth at the expense of his lie? Did the soldier possibly possess honest ignorance when he crowned Jesus with thorns? I wonder.

But, some Roman soldiers redeemed themselves. Here is the story of the martyred 39 Roman soldiers. "According to Basil, thirty-nine soldiers who had openly confessed themselves Christians were condemned by the prefect to be exposed naked upon a frozen pond near Sebaste on a bitterly cold night, that they might freeze to death.

One of the guards who set to keep watch over the 39 martyrs saw at this moment a supernatural brilliancy overshadowing them and at once proclaimed himself a Christian, threw off his garments, and joined the remaining thirty-nine. Thus, the number of forty martyrs were accounted for.

At daybreak, the 40 stiffened bodies of the confessors, which still showed signs of life, were burned and the ashes cast into a river. They collected the precious remains, and the relics were distributed throughout many cities; in this way, veneration of the Forty Martyrs became widespread, in the Republic of the Roman Empire.

The Republic of the Roman Empire run by elected Senators lasted for 500 years until the Barbarians came to clean the city from the filthiest <u>sin of the flesh</u> in all forms of adulteries, be they ordinary people, gay, lesbians, transgender, etcetera (not surprising which is becoming more common sight on iPad today).

If the 200-year-old America is railing on murders and adulteries read of Jesus' name, Saints and churches how could it last 500 years of existence?

A Saint said, I read, souls fell by the thousands into the fire of Hell every minute. Then think, how much more when they have their bodies on the day of Resurrection (our Credo), the pain of Hell then is incomprehensible which never lasts. Padre Pio once said smiling before an unbeliever, "If you do not believe in Hell you will believe it when you will be there."

❋

By: C. O. Abear

"LOVE THY NEIGHBOR AS THY SELF"

Hello My Father on Earth,

Let me share a story that happened to me, which may never happen again.

Tonight, while in a heavy downpour, working and driving my patrol car, I chanced on a red old Mazda minivan, seemingly stalled right in the middle of the entrance driveway of the Computer Tech campus, the vast four block property that I patrol. Heavy downpour was going on, so visibility was poor. The stalled vehicle in the middle of a driveway was an accident waiting to happen. So, in order to avoid incoming cars colliding with the stalled minivan, I positioned my vehicle to be visible with all the yellow amber lights blinking to warn incoming traffic of the stalled vehicle. When I checked the vehicle for occupants it was empty. I remembered earlier hearing over our security radio warning that a lady driver has left her vehicle as it has ran out of gas. So, I positioned my patrol car with warning lights blinking right in the rear of the stalled minivan while heavy rain not seen in many years was soaking everything in the open.

It did not take long, when I noticed a tall white lady in her mid 30's standing beside the stalled minivan's door and struggling to open it. She was having a hard time holding a small umbrella in one hand while holding

117

a baby stroller. I got out of the car wearing my heavy jacket with hood and approached her to help. To my shock there was a toddler about 2 years old sitting in the stroller. I held the tiny umbrella over their heads, as the mom (I assumed) picked up the kid and placed him in the car seat behind the driver's seat. The toddler is curly and chubby and was just wearing light shirt and diaper. The mom told me that her cell phone is not working and that she and the kid walked 4 blocks down to the gas station to make a call for road side assistance and then had to walk back. I said to myself, what? Walking with a kid in the stroller four blocks and back under the heaviest downpour in many years? Walked in the cold lonely dark street of the night? My heart sank for this mother and son. How difficult it must have been.

The mom told me that the road side assistance has been contacted and was coming. So, they sat there in their old minivan, mom and son cold and wet, waiting. I left them and continued on with my patrol then a voice tells me, "They are hungry." So, I turned around to give them the only food left in my lunch box, an apple. I motioned her to lower her driver side window and I offered her the apple which surprised her judging from her looks. Maybe she did not expect that someone in the middle of the rain would offer her an apple. She readily took it. She must have been hungry.

I resumed patrolling, then the voice comes again telling me, "It is cold in the van." So, I thought of the free-flowing coffee and chocolate drink in the company cafeteria. I parked my vehicle, got out and went inside the building to get the hot chocolate. I drove back to her, again motioned her to roll down the window and offered her the hot chocolate. She was again surprised and I saw in her hand the apple I gave her earlier; half of the apple was gone. She was hungry. I am sure, she shared it with the baby.

Another hour has passed and no road side assistance has shown up. I checked on them and the mom was a face of resignation and the cute curly haired toddler was standing on the front passenger seat, leaning on his mom, smiling at me. It was a heart melting smile. I told the mom that I will buy her gas on my break if the road side assistance has not come yet. They must have been sitting in the van for 3 hours now.

Thirty minutes after, I took my break, drove my car to the gas station, purchased a fuel plastic container and filled it with a gallon of gas. Paid about $13.00 all together.

She was still there when I arrived with my fuel container. Then I suddenly realized that I may end up having a problem by violating our company policy, "Hands off on peoples' vehicles." This policy is to avoid liability issues against security officers who may attempt to fix cars in trouble. And I was pretty sure that building surveillance cameras were looking down at us. This time, I was already joined by two other officers. I asked the most senior officer what to do since we were on camera. She said, go ahead anyway. So, I opened the minivan's gas port, poured in half of the gallon of fuel only as it was going down slow and eating our work time. She should have more than enough to reach the closest gas station. The car had a hard start and the engine came to life. We were relieved to hear the engine kicked to life, and the mom was so expressive of how good we were and that she never expected people could come and help them.

Judging from how they looked, the mom simple, thin and weather beaten face, a cell phone that has no signal (line cut?), old faded car, and boxes and clothes inside; my impression was these mother and son were very far from being well off. Or were they living off in this old minivan? I may never know their real circumstance, but this I know they were cold, hungry, and needed gas.

When they left, I felt so elated and the feeling of joy was beyond description. I felt the love of God either from me to Him or from Him to me intensified. I was on cloud nine. My heart just burst with the love for God. Was it a small sample of what joy in heaven could be?

With the minivan gone, the three of us started to worry about our company policy violation. There would be three officers reprimanded before the shift is over, we thought. I was sorry I dragged the other officers into this.

Now here comes the reckoning. Remember I said we were on camera helping out the poor mom and son? And that our superiors could have been watching us? Later that night at the end of shift reporting, I was the last officer to come in the office. I slowly sneaked in to clock out when my boss, Mr. Jones called out my name. I said to myself, now I am in trouble. I turned around and looked in his face, he looked serious. I thought I am dead. I was ready to accept my fault.

Mr. Jones, asked, "How much did it cost you to help that mom and son?" I said, "One apple was free. One cup of hot chocolate was free." Mr. Jones said, "So you got her a chocolate from the cafeteria? "Yes," I replied. I added, "$13.00 for the gas and container. I gave her the container, too."

I was expecting a reprimand, but Mr. Jones said,

"That mom and kid were lucky, they encountered their angel tonight."

No reprimand. It was his call. My eyes welled up.

In my heart, Jesus' commandments resonated; Love thy neighbor as thy self. Whatever you do to the least of your brethren, you do unto me. Lastly, faith and love without work is dead.
Thank you, Holy Spirit, for being in my heart when you melted it with pity upon seeing the poor woman and her child wet, cold, and hungry in their stalled minivan. Thank you for allowing your love to be expressed through me by helping them as angels would have.

Love,
Son on Earth

P.S. Later that night, I prayed hard to God to keep the mom and son warm and safe.

LETTER OF TREMENDOUS TRIFLES

Dear Uncle Elmer,

My comment about your article which said that none of the 11 brothers (you, Tio Elmer lucky to be alive at 79) died of violence. Yes, the Lord covered all of them with His grace through our Mother in Heaven, Mama Mary. Your Papa and Mama's prayer were heard.

As I recall, it could have been Tyo Litong (becoming victim of violence) as he was always conditioned to fight and had the propensity to start trouble. Uncle Loreto had many several scary fights, some in dark corners of the night.

Another most likely to die of violence was Papa, your Brod Cesar, being a policeman in the midst of NPA assassinations in the 70's and the mid 80's.

There were daily killings of lawmen in Davao in the late 70's and in the 80's. NPA rebels were gaining strong support from the MASA, a grass roots movement because of their hatred against Dictator Marcos, the oppressive and cruel Dictator who was known that when he was born there was darkness and "laughing" of the demons.

I remember a group picture of Papa and other police officers (I knew them all) and these officers all were killed by the NPAs one by one. And I thought it was just a matter of time before they would get him. Papa was never afraid of anyone. He was more concerned of missing his Mahjong sessions.

Hence, I conditioned my mind to lose Papa anytime so when it happens, it would be less painful to bear, this man I loved and cherished so much.

At times, when we were together we were like cowboys, guns on waist ready to shoot anyone moving suspiciously. Did you know that I caused the death of 2 young men (NPAs) who threatened to kill us if we did not give tax to them? To keep the story short:

Papa was in Manila for an officer's training when I got an extortion letter signed by the New People's Army (communist guerrillas) local command in Davao. So, I decided to meet and give them money with the intention of asking them not to extort from us anymore.

But before meeting them, I went to the police camp to ask for an escort. Five cops came with me all loaded for battle. I briefed the cops about my intention; me giving the NPA the money, and that I just wanted to be safe and go home. No trouble intended as I realized later that my plan was so naive.

I had an envelope readied with one hundred pesos (big money at that time) for the NPAs. I had another driver in Papa's car with 2 cops hiding. Papa's driver would initially meet with the NPAs, then I would show up to talk to them.

The NPAs met us in front of Buhangin market at 6 pm. The market was bustling with people. The three other cops were hiding in my car. When the NPAs showed up with their pistols, my cop escorts instantly reacted, jumped out from the car, and shot them in front of me. One died instantly and one wounded begged for his life but they finished him off anyway. Two guns and a grenade were recovered from them.

After that event, 4 of 5 cops who were with me were assassinated out of vengeance. And everyday, I expected an assassin to come and get me. So, I armed myself to the teeth and promised that I would at least bring one of them with me to the death. This event had changed my outlook in life and I was never the same again.

That shooting incident in front of a multitude of people in the market place made news headlines for 2 weeks. *Samut kasikat* ang mga Abear. The killing of those two poor guys was a closed book. A classic example of Police vs NPA encounters. Looking back, I came to realized that I suffered from Post-Traumatic Stress Disorder. I never consulted a doctor about it, I suffered long and in silence. Out from that experience, I became very susceptible to anger and was just ready to pounce on anyone.

That happened on June 11, 1984. It has been 33 years past and by God's grace I am still alive. I know He has plans for me; but to tell you frankly, I don't know what God has in mind. But what I do know, God has made circumstances to bring us (my family) together in the

U.S., saved for my eldest son who has a happy family in the Manila.

Papa was loved by God that he was given the chance to amend his short comings in life and that he died doing what he loved, playing mahjong. Maybe Papa lost more than he gained. I guess, playing mahjong as a past time was not as important as having a good time playing with his friends.

An Epitaph to remember before I end my story. A legion of Angels could have saved Jesus before he was crucified (Mathew 26: 52, 53) but for the sake of our salvation he deferred it that we might enjoy a Happy Life everlasting. Jesus, himself said, a Happiness in heaven beyond your comprehension.

In that order, Jesus said, "*Put the sword back into the scabbard because for those who live by the sword shall perish by the sword.*" In my case, the killing of the two young men in the course of defending myself was an act of preserving the precious life God gave me. This may not be an acceptable reason for the respective families of the two young men, but maybe in eternity we will understand God's mysterious ways.

God be praised.

Your Nephew,
Cesar O. Abear

*****

Dear Nephew,

I think your Grandma's daily Rosary saved him. As the late Dr. Aurora Minoza wrote to me once, *"There are more things wrought by prayers more than this world dreams of."*

Do you know that your Papa saved your uncle Jesus who was standing against Marcos as a Vice Mayor politician in Mati, Davao by him not to kill Brod Jess? His friend co-lawyer was against Pres. Marcos and was assassinated.

This lawyer's body was crucified dead on Mati's park with his penis half inside his mouth. The Nuns around whose school was near the Park seemed scared to see his penis "which was probably in the wrong place."

The Dictator was a very brilliant lawyer that he was able to mislead the President of the United Sates at that time to whom he made him believe there was a communist takeover. Ferdie Marcos had a very brilliant career, as bright as the Demons that had he chose to use his talent, betrayed the devil as St. Peter did not he could have been another Dr. Jose Rizal rather than for him to create a hero like Benigno Aquino.

As some people do (like you and me sometime) we choose the small devil often for the vanity of the pleasure of self. Too often we overcome it because our Angels are bigger than the Devils. I think, more powerful than all Hell, heh, heh. Alleluia!

Love,
Uncle Elmer

THE SOUND OF SILENCE

As this world is turning on its axis it expresses forth the sound of silence at every break of dawn.

And so is a living heart expresses the sound of silence between every beat to sustain its own life.

By every air a creature breathes the lungs pause for the sound of silence to emit.

What is this, sound of silence? But the image and likeness of God, his kingdom that dwells upon us.

✻

A MATTER OF FAITH
Upon Endless Shoreline

After Christ is buried
today not yesterday in Vatican

Some red cap apostles go back
on dry canoeing business.

Two millennium is a song
without syllables, neither notes.

And the selfsame routine,
becomes an endless footprints on

endless shoreline...
Surely this time high tide comes

has seen as Ghost which reminds them
of the vanity of their canoeing business.

As ageless as Paul, the 2nd jumps ship
shouting at Manila's 3 million youth:
"It is the Lord!"

❋

IN REMEMBRANCE

I remember the day I walked
my loved pets on Ogdensburg's
wooden bridge, they shouted-

"What's wrong old blind man
that we so love, wavering more
into the river's left dark side?"

I remember I saw a light that shone
in my darkness, after Christ's blessing.
Though wavering with delight

 I found an Inn for a good
dark night rest, i said:
"Thank you, Lord, have a nice day."

❋

MY HEART & MIND

There are a lot of mockingbirds
within my confused mind.
Mocking my useful toil
and hence, I'm deprogramed.
Deregulated and diminished what seems
a holy fire of my being.

Yet, there are a lot of multicolored roses too
within my heart
that deodorizes my filthy soil.
Plows open a sore, a wound,
for the Eye of Heaven
to look at and perhaps mend.

When my heart & mind do meet,
at some disputed corner of my soul
a blessing from above passes them by
(Where once they felt so bitter,
they dared not speak)
Now, they sing in one voice, "Alleluia"
On the way to the Cross.

✻

REJOICE

Life had become usual,
Thomas thought.

He was sorry for Christ,
another good prophet like Elijah
got busted.

To be one united with his fishermen buddies
he was with them in the upper room.

Then Jesus just passed through the closed doors
and Thomas brushed his eyes lest he was seeing a ghost.

He called out, "Thomas touch my hands,
my wound on my right side."

Still doubting the words of Christ,
he went and touched and his soul was uplifted up
with heavenly joy.

He knelt down and said,
"My Lord and my God."

❄

A VOICE IN THE RAIN
Ddt. to Roy-Babette Escudero

When Summer drought 2012 came
to St. Laurence County, dandelions
were the only green that decorated
my dead lawn and waved yellow
flowers to brighten my dropping spirit:
they have just overcome for me
the tribulation of heat like Hades.

I wonder where they got their
inspiration, strength, and nourishment
when for weeks there was not a drop of rain.
I wonder still what intention they have when
amidst the rain last Summer, they gently
elbowed the beauty of my red roses
out of sight behind wild leaves in hiding.

Now, I am informed by the rain expression
about the martyrdom of self and learn
how to sacrifice the red roses I have
and try to listen to the voice in the rain
that I might have the insight
to see what glory Heaven must be like
without rain or Hades in site.

❋

SONNET 666

Her name was Al Sheba Anopheles
Who came out in hiding
From the jungle of Mindanao.

In the twilight of his bedroom
She saw his
bare but Christian open arm.

Like a thief in the night
She made a soft landing
And drained away his blood…

For what she took away,
His life and all
It gave birth to a new man.

✻

THE FRANCISCANS

St. Francis of Assisi was
Physically like me
A short and ugly loving person.

Yet, they carved him,
As handsome as he could possibly be
A tall statue in my chapel room.

Maybe, I thought,
That through him they were made holier
by his prayer.

On his right sat,
A menacing but sort of kind
brown looking Doberman.

Between its contrast
Their shadows seemed to have fallen
By his light on my mind.

With this triune image hovering
I wonder where I belong,
Even they, even you, even me.

❋

A MIND IN AUTUMN

Ddt. To the late Ano A. Minoza

His mind in Autumn was gradually slipping into a faraway land whose journey no travelers returned.

By the last tick of his mind's clock something had happened: His loved ones thought, he lost his mind,

As if dried rose-petals had gracefully fallen, from inside his brain. In the garden of a no man's land.

Past, present, and future had gracefully become void, in the sea way trail of his Alzheimer's mind.

❄

NOTE: Published in the *Philippines Free Press,* March 2012

WHEN YOUR PRAYER
DOES NOT SEEM TO WORK

When your prayer does not seem to work, forget yourself for a while, and try to pray for others instead. Sound strange?

Remember, the scene when Jesus was preaching inside a house? Some of those people listening to Jesus must have remembered a sick man in their community. And knowing Jesus had power over the sick, they went out to fetch this paralyzed man.

I reasonably assume, that this man must have been paralyzed either form birth, or had a fall or was hit by a polio virus. Whatever the case might have been, we could all agree on one thing: the man was paralyzed.

It is highly possible that this particular man never asked to be cured, when Jesus was around. First, most paralyzed persons often think that their cases are hopeless. This particular man was no exception. He became a member of the "potato couch."

Or second, this paralyzed man might have never prayed or asked to be cursed because like Mo. Angelica of the ETWN, it was a sort of protection or him from the evil ones. Faith freezes, you know, any types of decadence. Status quo became the order of life in this particular man.

Be that as it may, a group of men convinced this man to be cured by Christ. These is no question, in my opinion that the faith of these men could be far higher than this paralyzed man. Otherwise, they would not bother bringing this man to Jesus.

Anyway, when this group of men arrived in the house with this paralyzed man they could not get in. The house was overcrowded with people. So, they opened a roof of this house and brought the stricken man slowly down to Jesus. I often wonder if the owner of the house agreed to that. I assume he did, perhaps out of compassion to this sick man.

Now, why did I ask you to remember this scene? I think, the action of these men to bring this sick man to Jesus was itself a result of their faith. For them, to bring down this sick man to Jesus was prayer itself in action. These men must have been convinced by Jesus when He said, "Love your neighbors as you love yourself." Praying for others is to love your neighbors.

❋

GROWING FLOWERS ON STONE

This is a true story. Noni, a good friend of mine in Newfoundland, who happened to be a biology teacher, was one day watering the flowers around his house.

He spent so much time watering on the stones that his neighbor could no longer stand and asked him: "Why are you watering the stones?"

"Because stones grow," Noni answered and added with a twinkle in his eyes, "And if I persevere long enough flowers will one day bloom on these stones."

With the look in his eyes Noni knew that he thought he was crazy and he said like a mocking bird, "Do you really believe that?"

"You wanna bet?" Noni challenged him

"You are lucky. I hate gambling." He answered.

When Noni noticed that his neighbor probably went on holiday in Canaque, near New York 1,000 islands, he started painting roses and tulips on stones.

Actually, he had thought of painting those stones with flowers as part of his house-decoration long before his nosy neighbors had asked such untimely question.

When his neighbor came back he was amazed to see beautiful flowers on stones, roses, tulips, you name it. Shocked and unable to speak Noni shouted with a smile on his face, "You see, I told you so."

✻

HOW DID MY NEPHEW, JUN, APPEAR TO ME?

This was how the story started. It was mid June 1995. We went shopping the whole day, and on the way home I remembered something.

"Guys," I said, "Did you buy my candles?" I got no response, and then Alona said, "We can drop by the Martin Grove Store near home. They have candles there."

Boyet parked right in front of the convenience store, and everyone rushed to the store except me. I decided to stay in the car knowing it would only take a few minutes for them to buy a bunch of candles. However, an hour passed, and I decided to follow them to the store so that it would expedite the purchase of my candles.

Before I could get into the store, a young man cut in right in front of me. He appeared to be in his thirties, wearing a t-shirt with long sleeves rolled up, a plastic bag in hand, and was asking for money. Usually, I would kindly wave him aside. But instead, for some unknown reason, I listened to him.

"I have been in the street and have not slept and eaten for three days. Can you help me?

Though he appeared well dressed and well nourished, his hair appeared wet, and his face did not look haggard,

I believed what he said. So out of faith and not out of reason, I went through my pockets for loose change – no luck; not a dime.

Hoping for a dollar bill, I opened my wallet and found one bill, a five-dollar bill. *Shall I give it or not?* I struggled within. I always struggled with money coming out of my wallet but not money coming in (a wisdom I unlearned recently.) Not fully convinced of what I was thinking, I nevertheless handed over my only five-dollar bill with a trembling hand. Being a fixed pensioner, I guess I was just nervous sacrificing that much money for a stranger.

Or perhaps I could not rule out the belief surfacing into my consciousness that every man, rich or poor must have an affinity with the poor as Christ did. I thought of Imelda and how she would respond in such situation. Would she react the same way i did? Then i realized that she was far more generous than me.

As the beggar accepted my money, he weirdly examined the five-dollar bill, lifted it, and viewed it in the sky. No holes, I guessed. I did not know what was on his mind – too small perhaps or too big money?

In my humble opinion, it was too big for a beggar. He stared at me and said, "Thank you," and left. *As simple as that*, I thought to myself. *My only five-dollar bill for my morning cereal gone for good. Alleluia!*

As I entered the store, out of curiosity, I glanced back at him. I saw no one. "Wait. He could not run that fast," I said to myself. I immediately opened the door and went outside. Not a soul was walking on the street.

I rechecked the credentials of my psyche by carefully looking on both sides of the street, one hundred meters on each side and beyond. Not a soul was lumbering around. This experience was clearly an evidence of my encounter with someone who was from the other side. In fact, the streets were empty of people. I could be daydreaming, but not my five-dollar bill.

Anyway, there was no question on my mind something had gone awfully wrong. Did my five-dollars vanish into thin air with him? I shook my head in disbelief and thought even Ben Johnson with or without the help of a steroid could not run that fast.

When everybody was seated in the car and we were on our way home, I announced to my gang that I saw a young fellow, a beggar who vanished into thin air with my money. They laughed, thinking I was joking. I told them to check their time – 4:30 p.m. – for an incident that might turn ugly some-where. I was sure 101 percent.

Well, after giving them the precise moment of occurrence and given the seriousness of my voice, I looked around for a change in their demeanor. As perhaps a sign of deep respect, they shook their heads and seemed to say, "Uncle Elmer was seeing things Anyway, whatever my mental state was on their fertile minds did not affect me. I always felt comfortable with healthy skepticism. It was nice to have the truth to yourself. And everybody else, by not believing, had unknowingly become a liar to themselves. The next day, Monday, we were back in Ogdensburg. I rewound our answering machine and heard Nang Lita's message for me to return her call. I called her, and between sobs, she told me that Jun tragically drowned and was found dead at around four o'clock in the afternoon. That was the exact time the "beggar" appeared to me. I was devastated but not anymore surprised. I prayed for his soul.

I recalled the event of that mysterious beggar yesterday, and I had no doubt that behind the veil of this beggar was my nephew, Jun. He was not asking for money after all but prayer. My five-dollar bill was not returned; I guessed it went to purgatory. Certainly, the owner needed purgation too.

I remembered how the beggar looked at the sky with the money. His focus on the sky confirmed my judgment as to where he is now. While this incident may be viewed by others as just a figment of my imagination, I experienced it as a fact of life that I had to reckon with.

POSTSCRIPT:

Nang Lita, wife of my brother, Ondo, described to me the day Jun left for an outing. He wore a long sleeved t-shirt and brought along a plastic bag with him. He would be going out for the whole day with his girlfriend with whom he was engaged to be married. He just got a good job and happy to start a new life for himself.

When I saw Jun Abear lying in state funeral parlor in New Jersey, I had no doubt that he was exactly the same person I saw that Sunday afternoon past 4:00 p.m., the beggar asking for money because he had gone without food and sleep for three days. Three days of suffering, day and night, just a few seconds after his death to see me. It made me realize the "time" zone between heaven and earth. Let me share with you what limited insight I have of the above event in order to make sense of this visitation by Jun and perhaps learn something that maybe bigger than ourselves.

REFLECTION:

First, it was indeed a humbling experience and witness to know for myself that Jun was definitely in purgatory. After his death (as everybody would probably undergo the same procedure, if God would allow) Jun saw the entire world in one perspective.

After death, we appear to regain our intelligence innocence, and angelic power that Adam and Eve lost for us in the garden of paradise, a place many allegedly believe to be located somewhere in the Middle East.

In my opinion, the serpent is no longer there, I am certain that the serpent has gone into the genes of Adam and Eve and has passed on to succeeding generations. Hence, man has become a composite of good and evil.

At the outset, what Jun probably saw was poor me. He immediately noticed that among his clan I was one of the persons who prayed constantly for the souls in purgatory. I felt humbled by Jun's choice to appear before me, and I will try my best to continue to pray for him.

I assigned a rosary for him and his cousins every Tuesday. And if I could do it after reciting twelve rosaries daily in honor of Mama Mary's crown of twelve stars, I would.

I enjoy the repetitious breathing air in and out of my lungs. If I stop breathing air in and out, my body will surely die just as surely as my soul will die without constant prayer. It does not necessarily take holiness to do this. It only takes love that even sinners like me could do. The grace of the Lord is amazing if only you will ask and co-operate with it. Peace is your reward.

With God's permission, he allowed me to see a beggar veiled in such a way that my earthly eyes failed to unlock his true identity Souls on the other side always catch us unaware of their presence. I've witnessed this on several occasions. From our Christian belief, handed down from St. Peter to the present pope, it is said that if a person dies suddenly without preparation but is in a state of sanctifying grace or is able to recite the "act of perfect contrition," his sins are forgiven for all eternity. But somehow, the scars of sins left after forgiveness need as Christ said, "No one enters the gate of heaven who is not perfect."

Rick Warren, author of the famous book The Purpose Driven Life, states that after death there are only two places to go: heaven or hell. He might have theologically overlooked the fact that no one dies perfect (unless one has lived an extraordinary life of holiness while on earth, life for example St. Teresa of Calcutta or St. Padre Pio).

After death, there is a place called "purgatory" where faithful souls would spend some time before going to heaven. Mother Angelica said in one of her shows that if she would make it to purgatory, heaven is the next stop.

People in purgatory desire to go to heaven while people in hell do not. According to Mother Angelica, if people in heaven worse than hell because they are the only unclean souls. However, contesting this idea using our usual earthly wisdom can only be done after you have died. And you can argue about it forever and ever.

Let us not forget that suffering in purgatory, which is almost like hell according to St. Faustina, could be shortened by the prayers of people on earth, most especially offering the most powerful prayer, the holy sacrifice of the Mass.

If you can save one soul in purgatory and lead them to heaven by your prayers, you can be assured of your own salvation. Hence, devoid of any presumptive motive, I constantly pray on a daily basis for the souls of the faithful departed to go to heaven, with the hope of my own salvation.

You know, let's be practical and be honest. I want to save my soul too. I do not know about you. Can I ask you to pray one Hail Mary for Jun? Thank you.

Last shot: Jesus said to St. Faustina, "The greatest sinner has the greatest opportunity of my mercy," like the thief on the right side of Christ on Calvary. With God's divine mercy, it is indeed much easier to go to heaven than to go to hell. God bless you. Alleluia.

A PORTRAIT OF A SINGLE MOTHER

PROLOGUE:

Today in America, about 60 percent of our mothers are single women. That is the truth in which we are all witnesses. Yet, being a single mother is not something new. In 1834, I know of a single mother in the Philippines who was the granddaughter of a Spanish priest.

Ana was her name. She was the most beautiful girl in Argao-long nose, white skin and brownish-blue eyes. She was known as the "wonder girl" in town.

Back then, people in the Philippines were not fuzzy about white priests impregnating young local girls because they improved their stock. Sin was not probably in the eye of the beholders.

In fact, it was considered by most a blessing from the high beam of the altar. I do not mean to justify the means but to proclaim that the mercy of God glorifies the end. In other words, God's mercy and love triumph over sin.

During those days, most Filipinos loved Caucasians because of their long noses, white skin, blonde hair, and blue eyes. Generally, Filipinos have flat noses and brown skin, a product of five mixed races. They wanted to have long noses and white skin, so they did not have to teach their children how to pull their noses every morning before the mirror to make them stand upright.

Personally, I had tried pulling my nose in front of the mirror when folks were away, but my nose just loved to squat like a frog in a wet marshland, a frog ready to jump at anyone who would make fun of "it."

However, the story of how Ana grew up, the concept of life she knew and scrupulously followed, was both challenging as it was intriguing in the environment that loved Caucasians and despised the Chinese race.

Let me get this clear: Filipinos and Chinese did not like each other during those days, not on racial lines but on habit of customs and traditions. However, until now, Chinese men could marry Filipina women while Chinese women were off limits to the "lazy boys." Generally, Chinese were dirty; Filipinos were lazy. Beside the fact, according to their unwritten custom, the Chinese wanted to preserve the purity of their race, something Hitler might have been misguided upon application. The skin's quarrel was a matter of preference rather than being prejudicial. Please get that right, and don't forget as you read the monologue below.

MONOLOGUE:

Now let me start this challenging and intriguing love and life story of Ana. This is a true story of a "virgin," either too good to be true or too bad that it happened. Given our present society of secularism, I would expect varied misinterpretations of facts and events.

Yet, given a society where this story took place, people's opinions during those days would be as transparent as their faith, crystal fresh but bitter cold like the first snowflake in Newfoundland. Nevertheless, this story was handed to me by word of mouth from my mother in 1945 when there was no TV or radio in Kansuhi (a mountain in Argao, Cebu). In the evening, mother kept us preoccupied with her stories prior to prayer time.

Those were the days too when mother was more precious to us than "prayer time" as we listened to her stories, some true, some fiction-but never fiction trumped with facts as in the case of *The Da Vinci Code*; no deceptive devices.

Of the several stories she told us, this true story has stood the test of time on my mind. Not only because the story is true-to-life in part or in whole (as I know) but because I can draw my strength out of my weaknesses whenever my life makes me weary.

In short, it has principled my life, cradled within an old creed of devotional prayers that I could not help but share it with you, if you don't mind. With underrunning reasonable speculations and literary art devices to enhance the effect, here is the story.

In front of my mother's paternal home in Argao, there lived a beautiful seven-year-old girl. To repeat, she had a long nose, dark brown hair, and white skin with a pair of beautiful, brownish-blue eyes. Get the picture?

She was a "wonder girl" to people around her precisely

because she looked different in a crowd superficially of the ugly and the fair. Most people said, "A gift from the pulpit in heaven."

The other reason why she was more of a mystic than a wonder girl was the fact that every time a makeshift hearse powered by two men with a coffin on top of it passed by her house, this particular girl would enthusiastically rush to her window and say, "How lucky that you have died! Lord, may I be next? Please!"

Since she dreamed to die at early age, marriage was out of the question. She would remain a virgin if she would make it to her teenage years, which she hoped not. She wanted to be with Jesus desperately, not as a nun, though how noble the profession is, but as a "single woman," a virgin for Christ's sake. That was her will and her desire.

When asked why she did not want to marry, her answer was she wanted to be with Jesus, Period. No explanation was necessary. Today, people like me would say, "We'll pray for you." But did the people pray for her? I wonder. I did not and maybe I won't.

She really believed she would die soon, at any given day. Yet, she saw nothing wrong with marriage, To be a nun like a priest for St. Francis of Assisi was too great a call for her to be worthy of. The truth about herself, Mother said, was her simplicity and childlike attitude no matter what the circumstances were.

Whenever she would get sick (though she did not refuse her mom's medicinal herbs), she hoped not to get well.

She offered her pain and suffering as her gifts to her Jesus. Though her wish to die early sounded morbid, she was not a depressed girl.

Depression was for the self-centered person. She looked at life happily as one more day to live. To her, tomorrow was a long wait, a very long wait.

Then, as days progressed to years, she became a young girl. She blossomed to be the most beautiful girl in town of Argao. Proposals from good men came and went. And like the song, "Mona "They just lie there and they die there" by the wayside of her virginal feet.

At night, whenever there was a full moon, many ballads and songs from young men died by her window. But the moon never fell on any one of them from the window of her own sky. She was the town's mystic and wonder girl.

But a man from China made her fall from the sky to be part of our humanity. Like Romeo and Juliet, they were very much in love with each other, but the town's morality at that time prohibited a Chinese from marrying a beautiful, half-bred Filipina girl.

Anyway, when this beautiful girl was impregnated by a yellow man, people got upset. They thought it was one step backward to improving their stock. Who should be happy with a smaller, nosy nose and yellow skin, not to mention the, you know, the eyes.

Oops! No prejudice intended. Just trying to express the transparency of naked truth to set us free from anger and bitterness and thus make us able to tolerate, love, and consider how miserable others look.

And so poor Mr. Tan was driven out of the country, back to China where he belonged. And unlike Romeo, he never returned to Argao. Besides, yellow skin was, although most Chinese thought otherwise. It had nothing to do with racism. Racism was not in the vocabulary of the Filipinos. It was generally viewed as a racial quarrel between black and white in America. To most Filipinos, I repeat, it was a matter of preference on one's skin rather than being prejudicial. Believe me; I am a Filipino.

Though this single mom wore a scarlet soul and became the butt of jokes, she did not abort baby. In spite of the social inconveniences, she somehow with all the Christian values she learned from the pulpit. She offered her suffering to God and bore her child as a gift from above with joy.

I think abortion during this time was almost unheard of. Gays and lesbians, probably advocates of abortion, were comfortable in their closets. I doubt if Ana knew the essence of their existence. It seemed that the heart of the town had the atmosphere of the "fear of the Lord."

Literally, it could be argued that the weather was not secular. A holy pope, though he had heard the conversation between God and Satan for him (the devil) to rule for a thousand years, had not yet seen the genesis of such darkness to come. In another word, the hornet's nest of the world was not on fire.

Meanwhile, she took good care of her only child. Though unschooled due to poverty, this child grew to be a strong and honest fisherman. Mariano was his name. And it was told later that whenever Mariano arrived after a night of fishing, people would meet him on the shore and buy his fish; if people did not have money he gave the fish away for free.

There were many nights after fishing that Mariano would comic home without a single fish to cook for dinner, and his wife would ask him kindly why and he would only answer, "I cannot refuse anyone who asks from me." And he would tell his wife, "Go to the market and buy some sardines for our dinner."

Mariano's generosity spread like wildfire in the town of Argao, so when the first election for mayor was held, he was elected with the greatest majority. Ana was very happy. However, Mariano felt bad about winning because he defeated a school's superintendent.

In the coming years, Mariano, called by people as Anoy, and Ciana, his wife, bore nine healthy children: Oliva, Juan, Antonio, Pastor, Pascio, Remedios, Theodoro, Sergio, and Manuel. All got married and had children. Juan, my father, was valedictorian with fifteen children. Oliva, Juan's older sister, had ten children and is the mother of Elnora Minoza-Mercado and Miflora Minoza-Gatchalian, Oliva is also the grandmother of May Ann Gatchalian-Kuik and Joel M. Gatchalian.

Nevertheless, Ana, supported by Mariano, continued to be a "wonder girl" inside her and perhaps before God because she never abandoned her childhood wish to die early.

And so, when some of her own people died each in their own time, their coffins passing by her house, one by one on a makeshift hearse powered by two lonely men on their way home to Jesus, she would be filled with envy.

Yet she was most happy for them to see Jesus ahead of her. Trusting God, in a childlike way, she was oblivious to whatever situation she found herself in. She was joyful in her life.

People could see her smile and could not understand the joy in her heart. As loved ones cried following the coffin, she could not understand why death should be da parting when being born into this world was a great joy. The band following the coffin had sad music that made people cry even more.

As she looked at grieving people passing by behind a coffin, she thought that if only their loved ones could whisper into their ears that it was not himself or herself they cried for but it was themselves they mourned for, it would certainly uplift their drooping spirit of Jesus, her Jesus. Anyways her wish to die early as the sun's breaking at the earliest dawn never happened. As roses faded and petals fell to the ground to the admiration of the torpid soil, she emerged after many years an old woman, dry in her smile but warm. Her wish was a dark shadow with no sun shining behind. She had nothing but faith and hope that burned through the dark night of her soul.

At age ninety, she was predictable.

She never missed watching happily every hearse passing by and saying to herself, "Lord, when am I going home? I love you and I want to be with you."

As she approached past one hundred years old, she gave up the idea of dying early, not out of despair or any sense of hopelessness, but because for her to die anyway seemed too late. On the average, people during those times died at age fifty-two, mostly from tuberculosis due to poverty.

Death, figuratively, had passed her by. All her friends at her age who never wished to die early in life had already gone to the other side. She had been in the pre-departure area (in the modern context) of her life with no plane in sight to take her home.

How she wished she could be with her friends who had gone to the other side. They only left their childhood memories when she used to play "Hide and Seek with them in the late evening, under the moon and among the glittering stars at night. The past was not dead to her after all. It often lifted up her spirit with the hope that tomorrow would be "today".

She was old now, very old. Though to the world she was like the former stem of a beautiful rose in Argao that did break to the force of earthly love, her simplicity and approach to life had made her holy in the course of her purgatorial life. She bore her life lovingly for Christ. In her simplicity, she now thought that God had indeed forgotten her--forgotten her for good.

Three calendars won't fit her age. She thought she was off from God's list. Though she thought God might have forgotten her, there was never a day in her life that she forgot to thank God for another day, another last day to live and cherish.

She could understand her love of God all right, but for God to love her was beyond her comprehension. It was as if she felt like a frog in a marshland trying to understand why she could not swim in the ocean beyond where the water was abundant and alive in the breeze.

Just when she gave up the will to die early because God forgot her, unworthy—she thought to be in his kingdom, the will of God came down like a thief in the night. Between her will and God's will apparently fell the shadow of God's sense of humor, Poor Ana died quietly on her bed at age 107. The generation out of her time was astounded but happy for her. Her long, sad, and happy purgatorial life had perhaps shortchanged her journey to heaven.

People rushed and looked at her, and they saw a beautiful smile on her face, Her radiance seemed to cast light in her room and threw an aura of her youthfulness that people could feel in their heart of hearts.

They could not understand that feeling. She was a town mystic (at least to some) but a human to be known and to be loved. Yes, she was young again, this woman indeed was a holy woman all her life, preparing enthusiastically every day as if it were her last day.

In her consciousness and awareness of God within her, people thought her weaknesses had made her a saint, for her childhood wish never faded, even in the best or the worse times of her life. In fact, it came back to her in adulthood as a redeeming force that made the length of her life seemed a short distance to heaven.

She did not read the Bible, for only the priest at that time owned a Bible. She only heard about Jesus from Sunday Mass when good and holy priests read the good news from the pulpit. People could not afford to buy a Bible, much less to read it.

Though literacy was in its infancy in Argao, the love of Jesus in the community where she lived was overwhelming—no people stayed in the house on Sundays. Stores were closed on Sundays; Sundays were reserved to thank God for six days of hard work.

San Miguel's church, built in 1786, was packed with people thirsty to hear the word of Christ from the lips of holy priests. Satan had not yet probably entered the holy place to challenge in a massive way the purity of the priests for "a thousand years."

She loved Jesus so much that neighbors said they could hear her singing at night and early down before the statues of Jesus and Mary and Joseph. Whenever she was asked why she sang her prayer, she said that the priests told her that the highest form of prayer was to sing. The early Christians, her priest said, "were singing while they were eaten by lions."

She said that whenever she was thrilled in her prayer she would not only sing but dance like those dark-skinned natives from the mountain of Cebu before the statue of Santo Nino before his basilica every mid January.

What was amazing on this day that she died was there appeared a white dove looking at her over the bamboo ceiling in her room. The white dove stayed there the whole three days while she was exposed on her bed clasping a rosary in her hand.

Yet the people knew that there were no white - doves in the whole town and even in the neighboring barrios. They believed the dove was an angel, a visitor and a messenger from God.

Since their belief was based on faith rather than on reason, they did not lose the argument like Adam and Eve to the devil. No wonder most people, if not all, had no locks at their doors. It was as if it was a community where the lions and the lambs had decided to sleep together.

Anyway, on the third day, when she was placed on a makeshift hearse for her burial, the white dove followed her coffin as two happy men carried the hearse to the cemetery. This was also the time when women did not do men's job, not emancipated, it seemed, from the cognitive beauty of their womanhood.

They believed she was an angel, a visitor and a messenger from God.

Nevertheless, the town's band decided to play jubilant music for the first time in many years. They knew from her radiant face that it was her long awaited day, her happiest day to be at last with her Jesus. The people began to understand her love of God and wish they too would like to die in an Augustinian way: "a little later, but not now."

After she was buried and a simple wooden cross was placed to mark her place on earth, the people started to go home. From a distance, they saw and witnessed for themselves that the white dove alighted on her wooden cross.

As darkness fell over the town, she flew far, far away until she was lost in the golden sun setting against the monstrance ovf the west. Her sunset was the beauty of a suppressed desire gracefully unfolding generation after generation of new stars while the old fogies like me are slowly fading hopefully into the bright light of eternity.

EPILOGUE:

Her spiritual legacy to be simple and childlike and to look at life as if it were her last day reminded me what Jesus said to his apostles: "Unless you are born again as a child, you shall not enter the kingdom of heaven".

While I was writing Ana's story, I realized that though I always prayed three hours before sunrise for all the souls in purgatory, between rosaries I could not remember I prayed for her. Maybe the white dove deep in my unconscious mind reminded me that this might not be necessary.

From this single mom, there came about a generation of doctors, lawyers, politicians, educators with PhDs, engineers, writers, simple farmers, nuns—you name it. Being the twelfth son of Juan Abear, I am proud of this single mom, named Ana (called Anang) Espina because she was my great-great-grandma.

WHEN SOULS DO COME FROM PURGATORY

One evening around ten o'clock, while Imelda and I were laying in bed in Bulacao, a young lady appeared to me out of nowhere. She was smiling at me. Though I have never seen her before in my life, I was not taken by surprise by her visitation.

As I gazed at her, she appeared like she wanted to thank me for my prayers (every day I always pray for the poor souls in purgatory) but also wanted to ask me to continue praying some more. So I said, "I'll pray for you," and slowly she disappeared from view.

As soon as she faded into the background, a white male in his fifties with gray hair appeared before me. He looked not sad but sorrowful. By mental telepathy, we began to understand each other's messages. All he wanted was for me to pray for him because nobody had particularly remembered him in his or her prayers years after he arrived in purgatory.

BLESSED ARE THE POOR

THE SAGA OF UNCLE PASIO

1. MONKEY BUSINESS:

This poor man is my uncle. I call him Uncle Pasio, In the dark forest of Kidapawan, not far from Mount Apo, where the largest Philippine eagles inhabit, Uncle Pasio had lived most of his life with his wife, Aunt Soling, and their five kids. Breaking the soil on this mountain behind his *carabao* and planting corn, rain or shine, were to him a source of great fun.

When my upbeat cousin, Lily, came home after a visit, I asked her how his place looked like, and she said, "If you brush your teeth early in the morning, you'll see monkeys grinning at you."

Such an image brought back my happy childhood memory of *Tarzan's Secret Treasure* to my mind. I was astounded. Tarzan in the Abear family? In his backyard was a small cornfield. The problem with his cornfield," cousin Lily said, "is that unlike human beings, monkeys would harvest his corncobs before they ever had a chance to get ripe."

"How did he solve this problem?" I inquired.

"One day, cousin Lily said, "Uncle Pasio turned his

radio on and placed it in the cornfield. The monkeys stayed away. But when the monkeys noticed that it was only a radio, they were back to their monkey business, harvesting his cobs at night's shift."

What was worse was when Uncle Pasio lost his only radio. He was so upset that the next day he caught a monkey, and the family had a feast for a week. Cousin Lily and I had a hearty laugh. Uncle Pasio, like the Philippine eagle in Mount Apo, had indeed become a "monkey-eating man."

Fortunately, or otherwise, I had a chance to visit him one sunny day. On my table was a nice, medium rare beefsteak. I ate to my heart's content, never tasted such a delectable food in my life; better than those served in Ponderosa Steakhouse.

After dinner, I asked him where he bought such tender beef, and he looked at me naughtily and said, "*Krrab, krrab, krrab*." (This is monkey talking!). I could not believe my ears! I had become a "monkey-eating man!" Until now, I was on self-denial for reason of sanity. Though I hated him, I loved him still, I did not know why.

2. PROFILE IN COURAGE

Courage runs in the generation of Anoy Espina Abear. Though unschooled because of poverty, the people of Argao elected him as the first barrio captain instead of a school's superintendent. His courage had kept the juveniles out of business. For his excellent public service, a street was named after him. Anoy was Uncle Pasio's father, my grandpa.

Anyway, the time for Uncle Pasio to leave the mountain had come. He was getting too old. Yet for him to leave this beautiful mountain that he loved so much must have taken a lot of sacrifice and courage on his part.

His children were grown up now and needed exposure to the civilization that he once knew. He wanted basic education for his children before they would inherit the mountain, the *carabao*, and the monkeys.

Besides, breaking the soil behind the *carabao* was no longer a great fun to him; his knees often buckled underneath his ploughshares. It was time to go. Arthritis was killing his knees, a gene in the Abear family tree.

Since Uncle Pasio and family did not have a place to go, he asked my papa if he could stay in our farm for good, and Papa said yes. Immediately, he built his nipa hut om the lot assigned to me as my inheritance. I felt kind of uneasy, I did not know the man. However, for Papa's sake, it was okay.

Of the seven brothers, Uncle Pasio was the poorest. After my father had spent his life briefly as Argao's mayor in 1945 and a merchant for thirty seven years, he retired and stayed in a thirty-one-hectare lot worth millions of pesos.

As a government official, he was not as successful as his first cousin, Titi Alcazaren, who became Pres, Carlos Garcia's Secretary of Foreign Affairs or his closest relative, the former Sen. Rene Espina.

"Did Uncle Pasio lose the opportunity to get rich? I asked my father, and he said, "Oh no. After he graduated at the top of his class, he packed his things, got a wife, and headed to the mountains. With his brain, he could have easily found the best opportunity for himself, but like the temperament of philosopher Thoreau, he just loved the mountains, a place he believed was titled by God for him."

After a few years, my father and four of his brothers passed away, leaving Uncle Pasio alone. With his good health habits, I had the impression that this man would live long. I felt uneasy at the thought, but I had no courage to tell him of his temporary stay on my lot.

One afternoon, he caught a Muslim red-handed up in the coconut tree stealing our coconuts.

"Boy," he said to me, "up in the mountain, my problem was the monkeys. Here, my problem is a human-monkey stealing our coconuts. He is lucky I'm allergic to human red meat."
When he demanded that he drop the nuts or else, the Muslim only laughed at him. Who would not laugh?

Uncle Pasio was so skinny, a slight breeze would blow him away. Anyway, what they could not settle in words, they decided in violence.

Though he unknowingly broke his left arm in the fight, the Muslim went home limping, perhaps with broken eggs, if he had any. Uncle Pasio, indeed, was equally as courageous as his brother, Nong Pastor, a purple medalist in the military and was Pres. Carlos Garcia's Malacanang guard. Of this fight, my nephew, John, told me, "Uncle Pasio forgot his age of eighty-seven and fought a younger Muslim of twenty-five and won."

3. A MAN, POORER IN SPIRIT

Uncle Pasio was not a religious man. In fact,

I thought he was a pagan—a good pagan. Though his wife kept some religious statues handed down from generations, he was not seen praying in the house, nor was he ever seen going to church on Sundays, except for funeral services.

I had the impression that perhaps, being a macho man, he thought that praying, going to church, or reciting rosaries were reserved only for old men and women who were probably afraid of hell. I never saw him say grace before and after meals.

Yet his life was honest and simple. In his heart, he only knew two commandments, not ten. The first commandment: "Thou shall do what is right for God's sake," and the second commandment: "Thou shall avoid what is wrong," and he added with a subtle smile, "for the sake of Satan," and we both laughed.

If he had enough money, he would go on biking five kilometers away to the cockfighting house in Toril City and gambled his last centavo. No one would question him in the house if he lost.

In the house, he was the envy of many husbands (including myself) because he was the undisputed, benevolent king. I would not mention "winning" because he seldom did "win" anyway. Whether he won or lost, he looked as if he were a happy man, unaffected by the adversities of life.

Discipline in the house? You bet. If something got messy in the house, he would line up his kids for the bamboo spanking. And if he could not get the truth he wanted, even his wife would have to line up for the bamboo dancing. He was not abusive. He just wanted them to walk tall, forthright, and straight.

In a nutshell, he was a happy and disciplined man. Though he was nearing ninety, he had no wrinkles on his face except wrinkles caused by too much smiling and grinning like those monkeys up in Kidapawan. He was never envious of well-to-do neighbors or keeping up with the Joneses. Neither was he envious of anyone poorer than himself.

I never heard him regretful of his poverty; nor was he bitter. He was always willing to help his neighbors if they could reciprocate his generosity. What he lacked in education, his courage and simplicity in life could confound the wise and perhaps counsel the foolish.

He had been in my lot now for years. Not planning to retire in Davao, I put my lot in the market. When Uncle Pasio heard about it, he passed the word to Joe (my caretaker) that he did not approve of putting my lot "for sale."

Uncle Pasio told Joe to inform me that it is an "unwritten family tradition that a lot owned by a brother goes to another brother." Period. No explanation was necessary. In other words, he owned my lot, and my only chance of owning it was when he would die because he had no more living brother to pass it on to anyway.

Since I did not want to mess with him, with my untested, self-taught judo skills being respectful to elders by "tradition," I thought that I might just wait for him to die.

But here's the irony. I was the one getting old; had my heart surgery recently in Syracuse, New York; and had been looking at life from the Jesuit point of view-to live life under sanctifying grace to the fullest on a daily basis. The future, they said, "is just an imagination and the present is all I have. "Did this mean Nong Pasio was all I would have? Not my will, Lord, but yours be done.

4. HIS SECRETS OF A LONG LIFE

Anyway, like Uncle Pasio, I wanted to live long. Take note: "wanted" is in past tense, (Not out of despair but out of supernatural hope). During my last visit, I asked him what the secret was of his long life. I asked that question not so much on my behalf but on his behalf.

To my surprise, he said that first, every morning when he woke up, he would thank God that he had not died in sleep during the night and had another beautiful day to live and cherish.

That was the only prayer he knew, just to thank God and try to live righteously. The details of the day he said were his gifts from God to enjoy. When he spoke those words of gratitude from his heart, his eyes turned misty, and he turned his face away. I could not understand why he suddenly became emotional while I felt nothing. Maybe because I was preoccupied and surprised at the thought that, after all, he believed in God.

Suddenly, I felt the great visitation of Christ from him as he showed me his kingdom. I remembered and understood what Mother Teresa of Calcutta said: "I see Christ among the poorest of the poor I indeed witnessed Christ in the least of this man named Pasio. And for the first time I realized the vanity of this earthly mansion in contrast to his everlasting home."

Nevertheless, you would perhaps understand my hesitation if I would say that at that time that there was nothing wrong with being rich and famous. However, I had to meditate along the "fault line" of my soul when our Lord said, "It is easier for a camel to pass through a needle than a rich man to go to heaven."

Maybe I thought that the reason why Mr. Francis gave up his chance of becoming rich and famous was to become the poorest saint in Assisi. He saw poverty like Mother Teresa of Calcutta (for the sake of the kingdom of heaven among the poorest of the poor) as the easiest way for him to pass through a needle and reach heaven.

Anyway, except when good fortunes came to me, I seldom thanked God faithfully on a daily basis. I felt bad that I thought of Uncle Pasio as a pagan but much more for myself as a Christian. I would not have known that if I did not experience the presence of Christ for me through Uncle Pasio, the poorest of the poor.

Christ was right when he said, "Never judge a person because I am the only one who sees the heart." Uncle Pasio's lifestyle seemed to have taught me the joy of walking on the most traveled road of poverty in the Philippines.

The second secret why he lived that long, he said, "I eat very little food." Without thinking (quite usual with me), I was quick to say, "Why very little food?"

And he smiled at my naivety and said, "Elmer, don't you know that I am a poor man? I have to eat after I feed my hungry family".

"Do you want to have plenty of food to eat?" I politely asked.

And he looked very delighted and said, "I would be very happy if you have some extra to spare, but just don't expect me to beg, okay?"

Back home, I was seriously considering to give him plenty of food. He had lived long enough that, though he honestly enjoyed his poverty, he deserved to eat plenty of good food, one "high" (HDL) in cholesterol.

Meanwhile, I made a new life's resolution: to thank God faithfully every morning on waking up and to eat plenty of food on my table "low" (LDL) in cholesterol. Cholesterol often confuses me but not a medium rare, tenderloin beef. Maybe if I eat little food on the table, my heart in sackcloth would perhaps be as good as Uncle Pasio's. So help me, God.

A BRASS SERPENT

After Imelda and I got married in 1971, we went to work at Mati Baptist hospital in Davao Oriental. I would have wanted to stay with Papa, who was sickly in the farm, but I had to work first to pay my loans.

Had Papa known that I made a loan for my wedding, I was sure he would have produced the money for me. Traditionally, weddings among Filipinos were the obligation of parents. But knowing how deeply indebted Papa was because of my education, I did not have the heart to ask even a cent.

Just when we had fully paid our loan and were starting to save money for ourselves, Pres. Marcos declared martial law on September 21, 1972-the first Filipino dictator to probably subvert the people's will for his own personal gain.

Given its mountainous terrain, Mali became the refuge of rebels fleeing from the capital. We felt it was not safe for us to stay in Mati, so we left to Binugao's farm, where I grew up, the home of the brave and the house of the coward.

"Thanks, my father," was my heartfelt word to Papa and Mama as we gave them each a good, warm hug.

"Oh, my favorite doctor," Papa exclaimed. We were most

welcome. A day to remember was seeing them happy and contented.

The following weekend, Papa threw a welcome party. The whole Abear clan came in droves for the food and perhaps for us. After all, we were the new kids in the block, Mama proudly announced that our stay was heaven-sent. For some unknown reason, I shook my head, something within my mind proudly rustled.

My medical studies took a heavy toll from my parents' limited income that they had given up some basic things in life. This I heard from my brothers and not to mention my sisters-in law. This day marked the beginning of my commitment. "I will serve them," I said to myself, "to the best of my ability. So help me God." Something within my mind moved a passing dark cloud.

Papa designed a cute, built-in clinic for me. It was not necessary for him to go to Toril anymore for his quarterly checkup with Dr. Galeos. He also did not have to travel this distance to have his prescription drugs refilled. I could do all that for him now.

I gave Papa a good checkup, Except for his blood pressure and mild arthritis, he was essentially in a fairly good condition for his age. He had slight edema on both knees, flaring up when (according to him) his good friend, arthritis, would visit him on a damp, wet day.

He was slightly anemic, so I put him on iron pills. Easy fatigability would rock him to sleep sometimes. And like me, he had dry, itchy skin. When both of us happened to scratch together, we would often say aloud, "To itch is human but to scratch is divine. And we laughed-like father like son-scratching our butts.

Unfortunately, I did not pick up on my medical practice. One day, I saved a dying man named Isidro from heart failure. Since then, my name started to get around. A patient whom I diagnosed as having a bladder stone was scheduled a week after for surgery. People began to flock to my clinic. There was light at the dark tunnel of my practice. I felt proud. And something in my mind just whined.

Since I was the only doctor in the area, I was often reminded by the saying, "In an area where everybody is blind, a one-eyed Jack is the King. To some extent, I said to myself, "In this area, I am da King where no quack doctor is."

What people actually did not know was that the man who was dying of heart failure had severe anemia, secondary to a civilization of hookworms in his gut. A doctor somewhere in the city thought he had heart failure because he could not walk ten feet without shortness of breath.

Shortness of breath was a magic word for the diagnosis of heart failure. And therefore, a patient should be spared from further lab exams that only added more money to the doctor's coffers. On a human level, I made no comment about the doctor's mistake. His gross error was my blessing. *Porya kaba* for him (free him from curse), or *porya buyag nako* (luck for me). There was silence in my mind, just awful silence in my glory.

The man with the bladder stone? Oh, I accompanied him to the hospital. Since he had no money, I told him to bring a fat chicken. By design, he saw me wearing the green gown for surgery before he went to sleep under anesthesia. I assisted Dr. Pacifico, my former schoolmate.

I remembered during our student days how Mr. Pacifico would love to barbecue fat chicken. Anyway, the operation was successful. The patient woke up understandably with me beside his bed. Dr. Pacifico got his fat chicken, and I got his reputation as a great surgeon. A great surgeon, *porya boyag*. Something within my mind just rattled.

The people in Binugao were poor. Since they could not afford my professional fee, I declared it free. Of course, I told them that I was not allergic to eggs, chicken, or bananas. Hence, chicken with bananas found their way to the clinic. I got a new name: Dr. Banana. Thinking about my new name, I went bananas with a smile. Papa used to say the mark of a holy man is his good humor. I was no holy man, but at least I could try.

Sometimes, not too often, I found myself chasing my runaway chicken round and round the house with my dog named Kokoy following me. If I would fail to catch the elusive chicken, I would have to settle for dried, smelly fish and soft rice for dinner. Life was simple, and it was great. There was a certain peace and joy in my poverty. My soul seemed to empower it.

Yet, from the other side of this bright life, I gradually

realized that my parents were getting old. Mama was seventy-two and healthy-looking, but Papa, at seventy-four years old, looked ten years older than his age. Ever since I could remember, since my high school days, Papa had been taking Indocid alternating with Butazolidin tab for his arthritis. He walked very slowly and with great pain. That concerned me.

He would often tease me, Elmer, you were able to cure others. Why can't you do the same thing to me?"

It hurt me to hear those words, not because it offended me-not in the least because I loved him dearly. What hurt me was my inability to free him from arthritis. Analgesics would just give him temporary relief. I shook my head, and for some reason I heard the rustle of my limitation.

Nevertheless, toward December 1973, Papa was getting sicker. His blood pressure I was able to control, but his arthritis was getting worse. He was beginning to have infrequent incontinence, and he felt itchy all over his body. He was edematous and miserable. I looked at the brass serpent on my wall (a doctor's emblem) and felt healed by what I did not know.

I brought him to the hospital for blood work so I could understand what was going on. However, all the blood work results came back normal except BUN (kidney) levels were very high. The med tech commented that the high BUN was a laboratory error and must be disregarded. Something in me rustled and whined. I became ambivalent.

Given the above data, after all my physical examinations, I came down to the conclusion that Papa's condition was due to the aging process, an academic tendency of the mind to keep apparently in store a brass serpent as mysterious as the fragrance of an olive tree.

As days went by, my impression of what was in store in my torpid mind gradually became more encapsulated. Any further investigations were simply an exercise in futility. "Let nature take its natural course, became wisdom of the world to trust, rely, and comfort my mind.

Hence, the idea of losing my father became unknowingly a brass serpent, a symbol of healing my own anxiety, concern, and frustration. So, the trappings of my life could go on. My life could go on. Then, my mind stopped, impervious.

I continued telling him the peace and beauty of the other side, that having educated single-handedly all his thirteen children, and having been awarded by Pope Paul VI as one of the Ten Most Outstanding Catholic Families of the Philippines in 1967, he should have no doubt of his success as a compassionate father to us. If he would live further, in my opinion, he might witness things that might undo his reputation and dignity. I could not handle that.

Perhaps Papa understood my skeptical attitude of his further stay in this world. I just wanted him to escape from this vale of tears to a more comfortable world. He smiled at me as if to assure me that the purity of my intention was well taken. Even though it appeared wisdom from "heaven," it seemed to run counter to the wisdom of the world, where God's will must be prayed and trusted.

In early January 1974 came the breaking news: we passed the ECFMG exams that qualified us to seek greener pastures abroad. I could not understand how I made it, Imelda was not near me. This was certainly bad news for my parents to hear.

But I had no choice. Life must go on. I saw the cutting of the umbilical cord and witnessed in my mind: the baby cried, rattled, and whined, but free he was. In my part, the vision was just my dream.

It was one fine morning, and Papa had just come out from his prayer room for his breakfast after his two-hour daily meditation, Mama, together with Mameng, our helper, was preparing breakfast for us.

Then I kindly announced, "Pa and Ma, Imelda and I have decided to leave for Cebu to apply for work abroad."

For a moment, Papa just glanced at me and meekly bowed his head to take a sip of his tea.

Tearful, Mama answered, "Are you going to leave your sick father? Who will look after us here in Binugao?"

This was a heavy statement. I was at a loss as to how to explain myself. I took a deep breath and managed respectfully to answer.

"Ma, Imelda and I are married". (This was by way of reminding Papa's dictum that "Once a person is married, he must be man enough to paddle his own canoe."). And I continued, "It seems I have no future here. I have to paddle my own canoe."

Mama, unable to finish her breakfast, stood up and cried in her room. I could hear her sobbing and wiping her tears away. Papa was not the emotional type. If he were, he would keep it bottled inside him. All the sacrifices he made for me for years apparently became an hour in vain.

I gazed at Papa, who said nothing, and his eyes got misty. He tried to hold on to his emotion, but, unable to do so, he gently wiped his tears away. His tears were like hard years that rolled by for a moment of my own dissipation. I could not stand it, I went upstairs, and I wept.

Weeks passed. It seemed the period of disappointment; self-denial gave way to a graceful acceptance. The hour of grieving had passed, and a new day for us had begun. We packed our things under mixed feelings of sorrow and joy, with Papa and Mama around helping.

We shipped some of our clothes and furniture. Although most were happy for us to go abroad, few of my loved ones saw it as an act of ingratitude and cruelty to leave our old folks alone in the farm after many years of austerity in their part for my medical study, and now this.

The argument was we only thought of our own welfare. Silence was my best argument. I just did not know how to get upset. Being upset was something I gave up long ago. I would rather be disappointed than keep the clock of anger ticking. I used "disappointment" for this occasion and remembered what Jesus said: "Pray for those who persecute you. Do good to those who hate you."

Toward late September of 1974 (a prelude of a stormy weather in August), the sea was rough. We did not take the chance, and instead we took the plane for Cebu. A few days after, we heard that the ship carrying our belongings sank in Zamboanga.

We overheard Sis Carmen saying, "Naga ba-an," (Curse to me for leaving Papa.) Being a former nun who perhaps had not fallen from grace for saving an essentially jobless ex-priest, her statement could be heaven-sent. For her to say that, she must have a good connection "upstairs."

Having lived my life "downstairs," I wished I had that connection so my word would be infallible. Something in me just grinned and gripped. My soul seemed to smell albacore.

So, humbly, I took that heavenly comment inside me with respect. Perhaps I needed more feelings of regret to ease my sense of guilt for leaving my parents that I loved so much, my papa and my mama. Somehow, I began to doubt if my parents ever knew that. Love, I thought, was not something I went on proving myself to others; it was something to live for in the art of daily charitable living.

In Cebu, we stayed at the house of my wife's parents while waiting for our placement abroad. After seven months in Cebu, we received a telegram that Papa was seriously ill and was rushed to San Pedro hospital. My heart sank. We immediately took a flight to Davao and rushed to the hospital.

When Imelda and I arrived, Papa was groaning with pain. But when I touched to kiss his hand, he knew I was around. He slowly opened his eyes, and his warm and radiant smile seemed to heal my soul, and I heard within my mind a vague delight rustling in the wind. His warm smile reminded me of the day he welcomed us in Binugao.

While Brod Johnnie (older brother, another doctor in the family) and I were seated in this room, he told me that while he was on his way home from his clinic in Calinan, he was overwhelmed with a strong feeling to visit Papa in Binugao. Upon his arrival, he saw Papa in a bad condition. (Papa had the gift of mental telepathy, but he used it only when absolutely necessary). I guessed that was the "overwhelming strong feeling" Brod Johnnie experienced.

Brod Johnnie also told me that a nurse gave him by injection solo mg. of Butazolidin few weeks ago that Mama bought to relieve his arthritis, my previous prescription that I seldom used and used it with great precaution. But now he was edematous and had severe anemia, running a high fever, unable to control his bladder, and he was delirious and confused. He immediately hooked up an IV fluid with diuretics. The next day, he felt relieved and apparently he was stable enough to go to the hospital.

Upon arrival in the hospital, Dr. Macapantay, a urologist and a family friend, was called in to evaluate Papa. After his thorough and meticulous examinations, he came up with the impression that Papa must have been suffering of chronic renal failure for perhaps a couple of years and recently became irreversible.

In his opinion, he should have been seen a year ago or at least six months ago where renal dialysis could have saved his kidneys, and perhaps he could have lived longer. Butazolidin should not have been given or even prescribed.

As I heard Dr. Macapantay's opinion, whinnying puzzles of might-have been situations began to take shape in my mind. I was there for two years in Binugao, noticed his infrequent loss of bladder, high BUN that I did not repeat, increasing itchiness of his body, easy fatigability, repeated Butazolidin injections-all wrapped up under the impression of an aging process, an academic impression that literally left him to suffer and die in the natural course of events.

At the end of such natural course of events, I began to feel what the rustle, dark cloud, grinding, whining, and silence were all about. I discovered in my mind a brass serpent of my own making unwrapped itself from its own trappings, and for the first time, I saw the naked truth of my own undoing. I could not stand it. I looked for a dark corner, and inside me, I screamed, "Sorry, my father. Sorry, my Lord." It was a long night in Papa's dying room.

Surrounded by darkness in my dark corner where my father was dying, I was awakened in the early morning of April 17, 1975. Papa was gasping between breaths and gesturing for something. We came one by one, and he gently waved us aside.

We did not know what he wanted until Mama came over. Though his eyes were closed, he knew the warmth of Mama. He embraced her tight to feel her warmth against the increasing coldness of death. Then, slowly, he gave up his soul.

And all the furrows on his forehead caused by the hardships in the life that he lived for us disappeared. He was beautiful in his death. God had spoken, and we all stood up and sang, "Immaculate Mother we come at thy call..." We started leaving one by one, each to our own world. We had seen a beautiful death, what God could offer to a man who truly lived a holy and uncomplaining life.

In the evening, back home, my sense of guilt was beyond me. I was on the brink of despair and loneliness. Suicide hung over my head like the sword of Damocles. For some unknown reason, I fell into a deep sleep, and I had a dream.

Papa was sitting at the back of house, and I was full of joy in front of him. Suddenly, he was hit on the head with a big stone that came over the roof of the house.

Unknowingly, Brod Loreto howled over. Papa suddenly died in front of me, and I woke up in horror.

This dream gracefully cast away the darkness of despair inside me. I began to see the naked truth of the brass serpent, and he had set me free, I was healed and had an overwhelming sense of peace, not of my own making, but from Jesus, who said on the cross, "Father, forgive them for they do not know what they are doing."

At last, Papa was free too to travel into the promised land in which few travelers had returned to tell the beauty of the place. He went, as Dylan Thomas would say, "gentle into that good night."

REFLECTIONS & RECOLLECTIONS:
HOUSE CALL

PROSE:

One midnight toward late fall in Lourdes, I got an urgent house call from mainland USA. Since house calls were often associated with great anxiety and sometimes tragedy, I had always made it a point not to be involved emotionally-not only that I might have a heart attack, but I needed a mind that was not clouded so my decision would be exact, precise, and accurate.

However, this particular house call was not what I routinely would expect because the scene of this dying patient had made my approach irrelevant to what I witnessed. There seemed to be an invisible visitor, an aura of light from nowhere in this darkened room. A very old man was breathing slowly and gently between moments of silence.

There was nothing I could do but watch and experience a graceful, dying old man surrounded by his loved ones, who were not weeping but seemed to wear nostalgic faces. I could sense they expected nothing from me but simply to be part of them, as I was in this beautiful community for years.

His calm, old, wrinkled, but radiant face reminded me of how beautiful he might have looked during his younger days. This dying old man made me see clearly the mortality of man and the vanity of youth. Indeed, I said to myself.

POETRY:

The green grass has unknowingly
Left him as of late autumn in the
jaws of winter with nothing
but dried bones and papyrus skin...
Mr. Woods was 9 years old. Poem by
Canadian poet/physician Dr. Ron Charach.

With my stethoscope, I listened to his heart. No heartbeat. Just a few minutes before, when he had seemed to resist his hour of death:

His eyes deep in his own chambers
refused the swallow of general darkness

With my stethoscope, I listened
for his heartbeat—none
It made me reflect that a man was created, not knowing his time of conception. And after he went through the journey of life, he was dying, not knowing the time of his departure. Someone out there greater than life itself must have known Mr. Woods' genesis and a new beginning after an end.

Signal a mind that could not
tell his own beginning
nor where the road to the Mainland ends.

REFLECTIONS & RECOLLECTIONS: VISITING ANGELS

A TRUE STORY

I never saw him, my brother Celestino, because he was born nine years before me. But Mother and Father still kept beautiful memories of him, and she often reminisced about him.

I liked Mother's memories of him because her eyes would particularly grow soft and tender every time she told the story of his early passing. When he was still a baby, both Mother and Father lavished their love on my eldest brother, Celestino.

"He was not the kind who cried when left alone in his crib, "Mother often said. "I used to leave him alone," Mother continued, "while I was doing my household chores."

Yes, Celestino was a good boy. He just lay on his back, gurgling, cooing, and above keeping him company, playing with him, Mother recalled.

Often, Celestino would hold his toes, count them baby-fashion. Whenever he was hungry, he would just cry a tiny bit, not screaming or bawling as most babies do.

Celestino was a good
boy... smiling at the ceiling
as if there were angels above him.

But Celestino, my brother, was never healthy. Mother gave him all her love and care. But it seemed the angels envied her for having such a wonderful baby. And Celestino gradually became thin.

When he was just nine months old, he became quite ill. Father called in Dr. Susing (the doctor who Christianized me.) But skill and the medicines he gave did not make Celestino any better.

Then, out of nowhere, they heard the soft ringing of bells, a hundred soft, tiny bells, which in the late 1920's were not yet invented. Father, Dr. Susing, some relatives looked at one another, unable to say anything; their hairs stood on end. They felt the presence of heavenly visitors.

The bells continued ringing softly, beautifully for about five minutes while all the time Celestino's little arms from his very thin body were up waving at the ceiling, Mother recalled. Then, the sounds died in the distance, and my little brother, Celestino, closed his eyes silently, quietly for a heavenly repose.

Father went out of the house with a lamp and looked around the house, the garden, the street. He saw no bells or bell ringers. There was nothing like that during that time.

"They were visiting angels coming to take Celestino away," Mother said in a whisper as she wiped away her tears.

A LETTER FROM AN URBAN HERMIT

1. My apologies for not having written you in a long time. I've been having some health issues that have restricted my movement lately.

2. The latest has been bursitis but thank God this is better now. I just have to be more prudent and not over do my physical exercise. I was just so enthused and inspired by my losing weight I could not wait to lose more! I'm such an idiot!

3. During Advent I was reading Fr. Alfred Delph and Dietrich Von Hildebrand, both talked about the WW2. Both inspired me and gave me a fresh outlook of Advent that I found very relevant in today's world.

4. This Lent I'm reading the latest book of pope Francis, a book on the Oviedo cloth and a new commentary on the Gospel of John. I've finished the first 2 books and I'm working on the third. There's also a 4th book I'm reading: "Journey to Carith."

5. This one traces the history and development of the Carmelite Spiritually. I'm truly being nourished and challenged by what I'm reading. Journey to Carith particularly echoes in my heart and helps me understand my longing for a hermitical way of life.

6. I'm calling myself an URBAN HERMIT. Where other traditional hermits climb the mountain and only get a distant glimpse of the city lights, I climb 31 floors in the heart of the city and get a glimpse of the distant mountains on a clear day (when pollution level is not so bad!)

7. Where others hear the rustling of trees and gentle breezes I hear the rushing of trains and traffic. Where others at night may hear owls and the occasional howling of a wolf, I hear the din of bar music and shouts of drunken people cheering a game.

8. Where others see falling stars, I see the glare of ambulances and police cars. But this is life here and now and God is here. I want to be a hymn of praise for him who is here, to contemplate his marvelous love for each and all.

9. Where others may see his glory in a blossoming flower shrub on a path I see the face of Jesus in the man rummaging through the garbage bin of the big condominiums. Yes, I too walk paths, but they are in the alleys behind buildings in this concrete jungle The Lord has placed me in.

10. Some people tell me what I do is dangerous! Hahaha! When one is afraid everything is dangerous. I fear nothing. I don't see these back-alley people as wild beasts waiting for a prey! I see them as my Lord and God waiting for my love to return the love he gives me.

11. Amor se paga con amor! I don't give them alms and

walk away feeling good. I give them my time, my heart, my ears, my love. I don't walk away. I befriend them and listen to their story. I allow my heart to be pierced and I carry their sorrow with me, their frustration, their broken dreams, their hurts.

12. Then I see The Lord and hear his voice in them. Then I know the gate of Heaven is here where we meet each other as humans, friends, brothers and sisters. Indeed, the Word has become flesh and dwells among us!

13. Needless to say my dogs play a great part. The alley people are delighted by their friendliness. Usually the dogs are the ice breaker.

14. Oh how wonderful The Lord is. My heart really exults in The Lord's wonders. These are not the passing fascination of flashing neon lights or giant screens, but the splendor of The Lord's presence in half lit alleys that give me the appearance of some ancient cathedral.

15. The stray cats perched on some ledge are like the gargoyles of Notre Dame. The stench of the garbage is like incense signaling the presence of the divine and sure enough from the shadows comes the figure of someone hunched over a cart pushing his/ her collected harvest and I see my Lord! Would that my soul be pushed to heaven this way! Oh, gate of heaven opening here below!

16. Oops Glio is now grabbing my hand. He thinks I'm taking too long.

❋

By: Jay Francisco

BIBLIOGRAPHY

Abear, E.M. (2009). *Gone? Communication from the other side.* Oklahoma: Tate Publishing & Enterprises, LLC.

Abear, E.M. *First Love.* Compilation of written articles.

Blessed Imelda Lambertini. (References about this Saint is taken from the Catholic Encyclopedia online).

Mother Angelica. Recalled from a 2006 Show in ETWN.

Padre Pio (References about this Saint is taken from the Catholic Encyclopedia online).

Pope Francis I. (References about the Pope is taken from Catholic News Agency Archive)

St. Faustina. *Revelation of Divine Mercy. Daily readings from the diary of Blessed Faustina.* April 13, p. 121.

St. Francis of Assisi (References about this Saint is taken from the Catholic Encyclopedia online)

Ven. Bishop Fulton J. Sheen (References from the 1950's NBC television network show)

ABOUT THE AUTHOR

Elmer M. Abear, M.D. studied Priesthood in a Jesuit Seminary, San Jose Seminary, Philippines in 1978; Consultant Editor, Escolapion, Cebu Institute of Medicine in 1970; Literary Editor-in-Chief, Southwestern University's school organ in 1966; Editor in Chief, *Mindanao Collegian*, Mindanao University, graduated, A.B. in 1969; English Professor, St. Michael's College, Philippines; 3rd Degree Member of Knights of Columbus. Author of 4 books. Married to Dr. Imelda Ramirez in 1972 and has 3 children: Rossana, Butch and Dave.

Cesar Abear, AB. spent 26 years in detailing and promoting pharmaceutical products for Zuellig, Parke Davis, and Bayer in the Philippines. Retired as a National Sales Manager. A Roman Catholic in faith. Member, Knights of Columbus. Currently lives in Sacramento, California, USA with wife, Abeth Lavina, daughter Mary Grace, and grandchildren – Alton and Alette. He has other two sons, Mao and Ton, and grandchildren – Alyana, Alex, and Aiden.

...very inspiring, funny, yet spiritually deep. Written simply from deep within his heart, the author compels the reader to read on and on. This is a must for all – young and old, regardless of religion, nationality or outlook in life.

-Elnora M. Mercado, Former Managing Editor, Asian Pacific American Times, Denver, CO, USA

Made in the USA
Middletown, DE
05 January 2018